MW00807422

DEPARTMENTAL DITTIES
BARRACK-ROOM BALLADS
AND OTHER VERSES

BY

RUDYARD KIPLING

AUTHOR OF
"PLAIN TALES FROM
THE HILLS,"
"SOLDIERS THREE,"
"THE PHANTOM 'RICKSHAW,"
"THE STORY OF THE
GADSBYS,"
ETC , ETC , ETC

NEW YORK
UNITED STATES BOOK COMPANY
SUCCESSORS TO
JOHN W. LOVELL COMPANY
150 WORTH ST., COR MISSION PLACE

CONTENTS.

DEPARTMENTAL DITTIES.

BARRACK-ROOM BALLADS.

OTHER VERSES.

Contents.

I HAVE eaten your bread and salt,
I have drunk your water and wine,
The deaths ye died I have watched beside,
And the lives that ye led were mine.

Was there aught that I did not share
In vigil or toil or ease, —
One joy or woe that I did not know,
Dear hearts across the seas?

I have written the tale of our life
For a sheltered people's mirth,
In jesting guise — but ye are wise,
And ye know what the jest is worth.

GENERAL SUMMARY.

WE are very slightly changed
 From the semi-apes who ranged
India's prehistoric clay;
Whoso drew the longest bow,
Ran his brother down, you know,
 As we run men down to-day.

"Dowb," the first of all his race,
Met the Mammoth face to face
 On the lake or in the cave,
Stole the steadiest canoe,
Ate the quarry others slew,
 Died — and took the finest grave.

5

When they scratched the reindeer-bone,
Some one made the sketch his own,
  Filched it from the artist — then,
Even in those early days,
Won a simple Viceroy's praise
  Through the toil of other men.

Ere they hewed the Sphinx's visage
Favoritism governed kissage,
Even as it does in this age.

Who shall doubt the secret hid
Under Cheops' pyramid
Was that the contractor did
  Cheops out of several millions?
Or that Joseph's sudden rise
To Comptroller of Supplies
Was a fraud of monstrous size
  On King Pharaoh's swart Civilians?

Thus, the artless songs I sing
Do not deal with anything
  New or never said before.
As it was in the beginning,
Is to-day official sinning,
  And shall be for evermore.

ARMY HEADQUARTERS.

OLD is the song that I sing —
Old as my unpaid bills —
Old as the chicken that *kitmutgars* bring
Men at dâk - bungalows — old as the Hills.

A HASUERUS JENKINS of the "Operatic Own"
 Was dowered with a tenor voice of *super-*
  Santley tone.

His views on equitation were, perhaps, a trifle queer;

He had no seat worth mentioning, but oh! he
 had an ear.

He clubbed his wretched company a dozen times
 a day,

He used to quit his charger in a parabolic way,

His method of saluting was the joy of all
 beholders,

But Ahasuerus Jenkins had a head upon his
 shoulders.

He took two months to Simla when the year
    was at the spring,
And underneath the deodars eternally did sing.
He warbled like a *bulbul*, but particularly at
Cornelia Agrippina who was musical and fat.

She controlled a humble husband, who, in turn,
    controlled a Dept.,
Where Cornelia Agrippina's human singing-birds
    were kept
From April to October on a plump retaining fee,
Supplied, of course, *per mensem*, by the Indian
    Treasury.
Cornelia used to sing with him, and Jenkins used
    to play;
He praised unblushingly her notes, for he was
    false as they:
So when the winds of April turned the budding
    roses brown,
Cornelia told her husband: — "Tom, you mustn't
    send him down"

They haled him from his regiment which didn't
    much regret him;
They found for him an office-stool, and on that
    stool they set him,
To play with maps and catalogues three idle
    hours a day,
And draw his plump retaining fee — which means
    his double pay.

Now, ever after dinner, when the coffee-cups are
    brought,
Ahasuerus waileth o'er the grand pianoforte;
And, thanks to fair Cornelia, his fame hath
    waxen great,
And Ahasuerus Jenkins is a power in the State.

STUDY OF AN ELEVATION, IN INDIAN INK.

THIS ditty is a string of lies.
But — how the deuce did Gubbins rise?

POTIPHAR GUBBINS, C. E.,
 Stands at the top of the tree;
And I muse in my bed on the reasons that led
 To the hoisting of Potiphar G.

Potiphar Gubbins, C. E.,
 Is seven years junior to Me;
Each bridge that he makes he either buckles or
breaks,
 And his work is as rough as he.

Potiphar Gubbins, C. E.,
 Is coarse as a chimpanzee;
And 1 can't understand why you gave him your hand,
 Lovely Mehitabel Lee.

Potiphar Gubbins, C. E.,

Is dear to the Powers that Be;

For They bow and They smile in an affable style

Which is seldom accorded to Me.

Potiphar Gubbins, C. E.,

Is certain as certain can be

Of a highly-paid post which is claimed by a host

Of seniors — including Me.

Careless and lazy is he,

Greatly inferior to Me.

What is the spell that you manage so well,

Commonplace Potiphar G. ?

Lovely Mehitabel Lee,

Let me inquire of thee,

Should I have riz to what Potiphar is,

Hadst thou been mated to Me ?

A LEGEND OF THE FOREIGN OFFICE.

This is the reason why Rustum Beg,
    Rajah of Kolazai,
Drinketh the "simpkin" and brandy peg,
    Maketh the money to fly,
Vexeth a Government, tender and kind,
Also — but this is a detail — blind.

RUSTUM BEG of Kolazai — slightly backward
    native state —

Lusted for a C. S. I., — so began to sanitate.

Built a Jail and Hospital — nearly built a City
    drain —

Till his faithful subjects all thought their ruler
    was insane.

Strange departures made he then — yea, Depart-
    ments stranger still,

Half a dozen Englishmen helped the Rajah with
    a will,

Talked of noble aims and high, hinted of a
future fine

For the state of Kolazai, on a strictly Western line.

Rajah Rustum held his peace; lowered octroi
dues a half;

Organized a State Police; purified the Civil Staff;

Settled cess and tax afresh in a very liberal way;

Cut temptations of the flesh — also cut the
Bukhshi's pay;

Roused his Secretariat to a fine Mahratta fury,

By a Hookum hinting at supervision of *dasturi;*

Turned the State of Kolazai very nearly upside-
down;

When the end of May was nigh, waited his
achievement crown.

Then the Birthday Honors came. Sad to state
and sad to see,

Stood against the Rajah's name nothing more
than *C. I. E. !*

Things were lively for a week in the State of
    Kolazai.
Even now the people speak of that time regretfully.

How he disendowed the Jail — stopped at once
    the City drain;
Turned to beauty fair and frail — got his senses
    back again;
Doubled taxes, cesses, all; cleared away each new-
    built *thana;*
Turned the two-lakh Hospital into a superb *Zenana;*

Heaped upon the Bukhshi Sahib wealth and
    honors manifold;
Clad himself in Eastern garb — squeezed his peo-
    ple as of old.
Happy, happy Kolazai! Never more will Rustum
    Beg
Play to catch the Viceroy's eye. He prefers the
    "simpkin" peg.

THE STORY OF URIAH.

"Now there were two men in one city, the one rich and the other poor."

JACK BARRETT went to Quetta
  Because they told him to.
He left his wife at Simla
  On three-fourths his monthly screw:
Jack Barrett died at Quetta
  Ere the next month's pay he drew.

Jack Barrett went to Quetta.
  He didn't understand
The reason of his transfer
  From the pleasant mountain-land:
The season was September,
  And it killed him out of hand.

Jack Barrett went to Quetta,
  And there gave up the ghost,

Attempting two men's duty
  In that very healthy post;
And Mrs. Barrett mourned for him
  Five lively months at most.

Jack Barrett's bones at Quetta
  Enjoy profound repose;
But I shouldn't be astonished
  If *now* his spirit knows
The reason of his transfer
  From the Himalayan snows.

And, when the Last Great Bugle Call
  Adown the Hurnai throbs,
When the last grim joke is entered
  In the big black Book of Jobs,
And Quetta graveyards give again
  Their victims to the air,
I shouldn't like to be the man
  Who sent Jack Barrett there.

THE POST THAT FITTED.

THOUGH tangled and twisted the course of true love,
  This ditty explains
No tangle's so tangled it cannot improve
  If the Lover has brains.

ERE the steamer bore him Eastward, Sleary
  was engaged to marry
An attractive girl at Tunbridge, whom he called
  "my little Carrie."
Sleary's pay was very modest; Sleary was the
  other way.
Who can cook a two-plate dinner on eight
  paltry dibs a day?

Long he pondered o'er the question in his scantly
  furnished quarters—
Then proposed to Minnie Boffkin, eldest of Judge
  Boffkin's daughters.

Certainly an impecunious Subaltern was not a catch,

But the Boffkins knew that Minnie mightn't make
another match.

So they recognized the business, and, to feed and
clothe the bride,

Got him made a Something Something somewhere
on the Bombay side.

Anyhow, the billet carried pay enough for him
to marry —

As the artless Sleary put it: — "Just the thing
for me and Carrie."

Did he, therefore, jilt Miss Boffkin — impulse of
a baser mind?

No! He staited epileptic fits of an appalling kind.

(Of his *modus operandi* only this much I could
gather: —

"Pears' shaving sticks will give you little taste
and lots of lather.")

Frequently in public places his affliction used to smite

Sleary with distressing vigor — always in the Boffkins' sight.

Ere a week was over Minnie weepingly returned his ring,

Told him his "unhappy weakness" stopped all thought of marrying.

Sleary bore the information with a chastened holy joy, —

Epileptic fits don't matter in Political employ, —

Wired three short words to Carrie — took his ticket, packed his kit —

Bade farewell to Minnie Boffkin in one last, long, lingering fit.

Four weeks later, Carrie Sleary read — and laughed until she wept —

Mrs. Boffkin's warning letter on the "wretched epilept."

Year by year, in pious patience, vengeful Mrs.
    Boffkin sits

Waiting for the Sleary babies to develop Sleary's
    fits.

PUBLIC WASTE.

WALPOLE talks of "a man and his price."
List to a ditty queer —
The sale of a Deputy-Acting-Vice-
Resident-Engineer,
Bought like a bullock, hoof and hide,
By the Little Tin Gods on the Mountain Side.

BY the Laws of the Family Circle 'tis written in letters of brass

That only a Colonel from Chatham can manage the Railways of State,

Because of the gold on his breeks, and the subjects wherein he must pass;

Because in all matters that deal not with Railways his knowledge is great.

Now Exeter Battleby Tring had labored from boyhood to eld

On the Lines of the East and the West, and eke of the North and South;

Many Lines had he built and surveyed — impor-
    tant the posts which he held;
And the Lords of the Iron Horse were dumb
    when he opened his mouth.

Black as the raven his garb, and his heresies
    jettier still —
Hinting that Railways required lifetimes of study
    and knowledge ;
Never clanked sword by his side — Vauban he
    knew not, nor drill —
Nor was his name on the list of the men who
    had passed through the "College."

Wherefore the Little Tin Gods harried their
    little tin souls,
Seeing he came not from Chatham, jingled no
    spurs at his heels,
Knowing that, nevertheless, was he first on the
    Government rolls
For the billet of "Railway Instructor to Little
    Tin Gods on Wheels."

Letters not seldom they wrote him, "having the
    honor to state,"

It would be better for all men if he were laid
    on the shelf:

Much would accrue to his bank-book, and he
    consented to wait

Until the Little Tin Gods built him a berth for
    himself.

"Special, well paid, and exempt from the Law of
    the Fifty and Five,

Even to Ninety and Nine" — these were the
    terms of the pact:

Thus did the Little Tin Gods (long may Their
    Highnesses thrive!)

Silence his mouth with rupees, keeping their
    Circle intact;

Appointing a Colonel from Chatham who man-
    aged the Bhamo State Line,

(The which was one mile and one furlong — a
    guaranteed twenty-inch gauge).

So Exeter Battleby Tring consented his claims
to resign,
And died, on four thousand a month, in the
ninetieth year of his age.

DELILAH.

We have another Viceroy now, those days are dead and done,
Of Delilah Aberyswith and depraved Ulysses Gunne.

DELILAH Aberyswith was a lady — not too
young —
With a perfect taste in dresses, and a badly-
bitted tongue,
With a thirst for information, and · a greater
thirst for praise,
And a little house in Simla, in the Prehistoric
Days.

By reason of her marriage to a gentleman in power,
Delilah was acquainted with the gossip of the
hour;
And many little secrets, of a half-official kind,
Were whispered to Delilah, and she bore them
all in mind.

She patronized extensively a man, Ulysses Gunne,

Whose mode of earning money was a low and
    shameful one.

He wrote for divers papers, which, as everybody
    knows,

Is worse than serving in a shop or scaring off
    the crows.

He praised her "queenly beauty" first; and,
    later on, he hinted

At the "vastness of her intellect" with compli-
    ment unstinted.

He went with her a-riding, and his love for her
    was such

That he lent her all his horses, and — she galled
    them very much.

One day, THEY brewed a secret of a fine financial
    sort;

It related to Appointments, to a Man and a
    Report.

'Twas almost worth the keeping (only seven
   people knew it),
And Gunne rose up to seek the truth and
   patiently ensue it.

It was a Viceroy's Secret, but — perhaps the wine
   was red —
Perhaps an Aged Councillor had lost his aged
   head —
Perhaps Delilah's eyes were bright — Delilah's
   whispers sweet —
The Aged Member told her what 'twere treason
   to repeat.

Ulysses went a-riding, and they talked of love
   and flowers;
Ulysses went a-calling, and he called for several
   hours;
Ulysses went a-waltzing, and Delilah helped him
   dance —
Ulysses let the waltzes go, and waited for his chance.

The summer sun was setting, and the summer
air was still,

The couple went a-walking in the shade of
Summer Hill,

The wasteful sunset faded out in turkis-green
and gold,

Ulysses pleaded softly, and . . . that bad Delilah
told!

Next morn, a startled Empire learnt the all-
important news;

Next week, the Aged Councillor was shaking in
his shoes;

Next month, I met Delilah, and she did not
show the least

Hesitation in affirming that Ulysses was a "beast."

. . . . .

We have another Viceroy now, those days are
dead and done,

Of Delilah Aberyswith and most mean Ulysses
Gunne!

WHAT HAPPENED.

HURREE CHUNDER MOOKERJEE, pride of
 Bow Bazar,
Owner of a native press, "Barrishter - at - Lar,"
Waited on the Government with a claim to wear
Sabres by the bucketful, rifles by the pair.

Then the Indian Government winked a wicked
 wink,
Said to Chunder Mookerjee: "Stick to pen and
 ink,
They are safer implements; but, if you insist,
We will let you carry arms wheresoe'er you list."

Hurree Chunder Mookerjee sought the gunsmith and
Bought the tuber of Lancaster, Ballard, Dean,
 and Bland,

Bought a shiny bowie-knife, bought a town-made
    sword,
Jingled like a carriage-horse when he went abroad.

But the Indian Government, always keen to
    please,
Also gave permission to horrid men like these—
Yar Mahommed Yusufzai, down to kill or steal,
Chimbu Singh from Bikaneer, Tantia the Bhil.

Killar Khan the Marri chief, Jowar Singh the
    Sikh,
Nubbee Baksh Punjabi Jat, Abdul Huq Rafiq—
He` was a Wahabi; last, little Boh Hla-oo
Took advantage of the act—took a Snider too.

They were unenlightened men, Ballard knew
    them not,
They procured their swords and guns chiefly on
    the spot,

And the lore of centuries, plus a hundred fights,
Made them slow to disregard one another's rights.

With a unanimity dear to patriot hearts
All those hairy gentlemen out of foreign parts
Said: "The good old days are back — let us go
　　to war!"
Swaggered down the Grand Trunk Road, into
　　Bow Bazar.

Nubbee Baksh Punjabi Jat found a hide-bound flail,
Chimbu Singh from Bikaneer oiled his Tonk jezail,
Yar Mahommed Yusufzai spat and grinned with
　　glee
As he ground the butcher-knife of the Khyberee.

Jowar Singh the Sikh procured sabre, quoit, and
　　mace,
Abdul Huq, Wahabi, took the dagger from its
　　place,

While amid the jungle-grass danced and grinned
    and jabbered

Little Boh Hla-oo and cleared the dah-blade
    from the scabbard.

What became of Mookerjee? Soothly, who can
    say?

Yar Mahommed only grins in a nasty way,

Jowar Singh is reticent, Chimbu Singh is
    mute,

But the belts of them all simply bulge with
    loot.

What became of Ballard's guns? Afghans black
    and grubby

Sell them for their silver weight to the men of
    Pubbi;

And the shiny bowie-knife and the town-made
    sword are

Hanging in a Marri camp just across the Border.

What became of Mookerjee? Ask Mahommed
    Yar

Prodding Siva's sacred bull down the Bow Bazar.

Speak to placid Nubbee Baksh — question land
    and sea —

Ask the Indian Congress men — only don't ask
    me !

PINK DOMINOES.

"THEY are fools who kiss and tell"
Wisely has the poet sung.
Man may hold all sorts of posts
If he'll only hold his tongue

JENNY and Me were engaged, you see,
  On the eve of the Fancy Ball;
So a kiss or two was nothing to you
  Or any one else at all.

Jenny would go in a domino —
  Pretty and pink but warm;
While I attended, clad in a splendid
  Austrian uniform.

Now we had arranged, through notes exchanged
  Early that afternoon,
At Number Four to waltz no more,
  But to sit in the dusk and spoon.

(I wish you to see that Jenny and Me
    Had barely exchanged our troth;
So a kiss or two was strictly due
    By, from, and between us both.)

When Three was over, an eager lover,
    I fled to the gloom outside;
And a Domino came out also
    Whom I took for my future bride.

That is to say, in a casual way,
    I slipped my arm around her;
With a kiss or two (which is nothing to you),
    And ready to kiss I found her.

She turned her head, and the name she said
    Was certainly not my own;
But ere I could speak, with a smothered shriek
    She fled and left me alone.

Then Jenny came, and I saw with shame
  She'd doffed her domino;
And I had embraced an alien waist —
  But I did not tell her so.

Next morn I knew that there were two
  Dominoes pink, and one
Had cloaked the spouse of Sir Julian Vouse,
  Our big political gun.

Sir J. was old, and her hair was gold,
  And her eye was a blue cerulean;
And the name she said when she turned her
    head
  Was not in the least like "Julian."

Now wasn't it nice, when want of *pice*
  Forbade us twain to marry,
That old Sir J., in the kindest way,
  Made me his Secre*tarry?*

THE MAN WHO COULD WRITE.

SHUN—shun the Bowl! That fatal, facile drink
　Has ruined many geese who dipped their quills in't,
Bribe, murder, marry, but steer clear of Ink
　Save when you write receipts for paid-up bills in't.
There may be silver in the "blue-black"—all
I know of is the iron and the gall.

BOANERGES BLITZEN, servant of the Queen,
　Is a dismal failure—is a Might-have-been.
In a luckless moment he discovered men
Rise to high position through a ready pen.

Boanerges Blitzen argued, therefore: "I
With the selfsame weapon can attain as high."
Only he did not possess, when he made the trial,
Wicked wit of C–lv–n, irony of L——l.

(Men who spar with Government need, to back
　their blows,
Something more than ordinary journalistic prose.)

Never young Civilian's prospects were so bright,
Till an Indian paper found that he could write:
Never young Civilian's prospects were so dark,
When the wretched Blitzen wrote to make his mark.

Certainty he scored it, bold and black and firm,
In that Indian paper — made his seniors squirm,
Quoted office scandals, wrote the tactless truth —
Was there ever known a more misguided youth?

When the Rag he wrote for praised his plucky game,
Boanerges Blitzen felt that this was Fame:
When the men he wrote of shook their heads
     and swore,
Boanerges Blitzen only wrote the more.

Posed as Young Ithuriel, resolute and grim,
Till he found promotion didn't come to him;
Till he found that reprimands weekly were his lot,
And his many Districts curiously hot.

Till he found his furlough strangely hard to win,

Boanerges Blitzen didn't care a pin:

Then it seemed to dawn on him something
  wasn't right —

Boanerges Blitzen put it down to "spite."

Languished in a District desolate and dry;

Watched the Local Government yearly pass him
  by;

Wondered where the hitch was; called it most
  unfair.

      .   .   .   .   .

That was seven years ago — and he still is there.

MUNICIPAL.

"WHY is my District death - rate low ?"
  Said Blnks of Hezabad.
" Wells, drains, and sewage - outfalls are
  My own peculiar fad.
I learnt a lesson once. It ran
" Thus," quoth that most veracious man —

IT was an August evening, and, in snowy
  garments clad,

I paid a round of visits in the lines of Hezabad ;

When, presently, my Waler saw, and did not
  like at all,

A Commissariat elephant careering down the Mall.

I couldn't see the driver, and across my mind
  it rushed

That that Commissariat elephant had suddenly
  gone *musth.*

I didn't care to meet him, and I couldn't well
get down,

So I let the Waler have it, and we headed for
the town.

The buggy was a new one, and, praise Dykes, it
stood the strain,

Till the Waler jumped a bullock just above the
City Drain;

And the next that I remember was a hurricane
of squeals,

And the creature making toothpicks of my five-
foot patent wheels.

He seemed to want the owner, so I fled, dis-
traught with fear,

To the Main Drain sewage-outfall while he
snorted in my ear —

Reached the four-foot drain-head safely, and, in
darkness and despair,

Felt the brute's proboscis fingering my terror.
stiffened hair.

Heard it trumpet on my shoulder — tried to
crawl a little higher —
Found the Main Drain sewage - outfall blocked,
some eight feet up, with mire;
And, for twenty reeking minutes, Sir, my very
marrow froze,
While the trunk was feeling blindly for a purchase on my toes!

It missed me by a fraction, but my hair was
turning gray
Before they called the drivers up and dragged
the brute away.
Then I sought the City Elders, and my words
were very plain.
They flushed that four - foot drain - head, and — it
never choked again.

You may hold with surface - drainage, and the
sun - for - garbage cure,
Till you've been a periwinkle shrinking coyly up
a sewer.

I believe in well - flushed culverts . . . .

  This is why the death - rate's small;

And, if you don't believe me, get *shikarred*

 yourself. That's all.

A CODE OF MORALS.

LEST you should think this story true,
I merely mention I
Evolved it lately. 'Tis a most
Unmitigated misstatement.

NOW Jones had left his new-wed bride to
keep his house in order,
And hied away to the Hurrum Hills above the
Afghan border,
To sit on a rock with a heliograph; but ere he
left he taught
His wife the working of the Code that sets the
miles at naught.

And Love had made him very sage, as Nature
made her fair;
So Cupid and Apollo linked, *per* heliograph, the
pair.

At dawn, across the Hurrum Hills, he flashed
  her counsel wise —

At e'en, the dying sunset bore her husband's homilies.

He warned her 'gainst seductive youths in scarlet
  clad and gold,

As much as 'gainst the blandishments paternal
  of the old;

But kept his gravest warnings for (hereby the
  ditty hangs)

That snowy-haired Lothario, Lieutenant-General
  Bangs.

'Twas General Bangs, with Aide and Staff, that
  tittupped on the way,

When they beheld a heliograph tempestuously at
  play;

They thought of Border risings, and of stations
  sacked and burnt —

So stopped to take the message down — and this
  is what they learnt: —

"Dash dot dot, dot, dot dash, dot dash dot"
  twice. The General swore.

"Was ever General Officer addressed as 'dear'
  before ?

"'My Love,' i' faith! 'My Duck,' Gadzooks!
  'My darling popsy-wop!'

Spirit of great Lord Wolseley, *who* is on that
  mountain top?"

The artless Aide-de-camp was mute; the gilded
  Staff were still,

As, dumb with pent-up mirth, they booked that
  message from the hill;

For, clear as summer's lightning flare, the husband's warning ran: —

"Don't dance or ride with General Bangs — a
  most immoral man."

(At dawn, across the Hurrum Hills, he flashed
  her counsel wise —

But, howsoever Love be blind, the world at
  large hath eyes.)

With damnatory dot and dash he heliographed
 his wife
Some interesting details of the General's private life.

The artless Aide-de-camp was mute; the shin-
 ing Staff were still,
And red and ever redder grew the General's
 shaven gill.
And this is what he said at last (his feelings
 matter not) : —
" I think we've tapped a private line. Hi !
 Threes about there ! Trot ! "

.

All honor unto Bangs, for ne'er did Jones thereafter know
By word or act official who read off that helio.;
But the tale is on the Frontier, and from Michni
 to Mool*tan*
They know the worthy General as " that most
 immoral man."

THE LAST DEPARTMENT.

TWELVE hundred million men are spread
About this Earth, and I and You
Wonder, when You and I are dead,
What will those luckless millions do?

"NONE whole or clean," we cry, "or free
  from stain
Of favor." Wait awhile, till we attain
  The Last Department, where nor fraud nor fools,
Nor grade nor greed, shall trouble us again.

Fear, Favor, or Affection — what are these
To the grim Head who claims our services?
  I never knew a wife or interest yet
Delay that *pukka* step, miscalled "decease;"

When leave, long over-due, none can deny;
When idleness of all Eternity
  Becomes our furlough, and the marigold
Our thriftless, bullion-minting Treasury.

Transferred to the Eternal Settlement,
Each in his strait, wood-scantled office pent,
  No longer Brown reverses Smith's appeals,
Or Jones records his Minute of Dissent.

And One, long since a pillar of the Court,
As mud between the beams thereof is wrought;
  And One who wrote on phosphates for the
    crops
Is subject-matter of his own Report.

(These be the glorious ends whereto we pass —
Let Him who Is, go call on Him who Was;
  And He shall see the *mallie* steals the slab
For currie-grinder, and for goats the grass.)

A breath of wind, a Border bullet's flight
A draught of water, or a horse's fright —
  The droning of the fat *Sheristadar*
Ceases, the punkah stops, and falls the night

For you or Me. Do those who live decline
The step that offers, or their work resign ?
  Trust me, To-day's Most Indispensables,
Five hundred men can take your place or mine.

DANNY DEEVER.

"WHAT are the bugles blowin' for?" said Files-on-Parade.

"To turn you out, to turn you out," the Color-Sergeant said.

"What makes you look so white, so white?" said Files-on-Parade.

"I'm dreadin' what I've got to watch," the Color-Sergeant said.

 For they're hangin' Danny Deever, you can 'ear the Dead March play,

 The regiment's in 'ollow square — they're hangin' him to-day;

 They've taken of his buttons off an' cut his stripes away,

 An' they're hangin' Danny Deever in the mornin'.

"What makes the rear-rank breathe so 'ard?"
said Files-on-Parade.

"It's bitter cold, it's bitter cold," the Color-
Sergeant said.

"What makes that front-rank man fall down?"
says Files-on-Parade.

"A touch of sun, a touch of sun," the Color-
Sergeant said.

> They are hangin' Danny Deever, they are
> marchin' of 'im round,
> They 'ave 'alted Danny Deever by 'is coffin
> on the ground;
> An' 'e'll swing in 'arf a minute for a
> sneakin', shootin' hound —
> O they're hangin' Danny Deever in the
> mornin'!

"'Is cot was right-'and cot to mine," said Files-
on-Parade.

"'E's sleepin' out an' far to-night," the Color-
Sergeant said.

"I've drunk 'is beer a score o' times," said Files-
on - Parade.

"'E's drinkin' bitter beer alone," the Color-
Sergeant said.

> They are hangin' Danny Deever, you must
> mark 'im to 'is place,
> For 'e shot a comrade sleepin' — you must
> look 'im in the face;
> Nine 'undred of 'is county an' the regi-
> ment's disgrace,
> While they're hangin' Danny Deever in the
> mornin'.

"What's that so black agin the sun?" said Files-
on - Parade.

"It's Danny fightin' 'ard for life," the Color-
Sergeant said.

"What's that that whimpers over'ead?" said
Files - on - Parade.

"It's Danny's soul that's passin' now," the Color-
Sergeant said.

For they're done with Danny Deever, you
    can 'ear the quickstep play,

The regiment's in column, an' they're
    marchin' us away;

Ho! the young recruits are shakin', an'
    they'll want their beer· to-day,

After hangin' Danny Deever in the mornin'.

" TOMMY."

I WENT into a public-'ouse to get a pint o'
beer,

The publican 'e up an' sez, "We serve no red-
coats here."

The girls be'ind the bar they laughed an' gig-
gled fit to die,

I outs into the street again, an' to myself sez I:

    O it's Tommy this, an' Tommy that, an'
        "Tommy go away;"

    But it's "Thank you, Mister Atkins," when
        the band begins to play,

    The band begins to play, my boys, the
        band begins to play,

    O it's "Thank you, Mister Atkins," when
        the band begins to play.

I went into a theatre as sober as could be,

They give a drunk civilian room, but 'adn't
  none for me;

They sent me to the gallery or round the music-'alls,

But when it comes to fightin', Lord! they'll
  shove me in the stalls.

   For it's Tommy this, an' Tommy that, an'
    "Tommy wait outside;"

   But it's "Special train for Atkins," when
    the trooper's on the tide,

   The troopship's on the tide, my boys, etc.

O makin' mock o' uniforms that guard you while
  you sleep

Is cheaper than them uniforms, an' they're star-
  vation cheap;

An' hustlin' drunken sodgers when they're goin'
  large a bit

Is five times better business than paradin' in
  full kit.

Then it's Tommy this, an' Tommy that,
   an' "Tommy, 'ow's yer soul?"
But it's "Thin red line of 'eroes" when
   the drums begin to roll,
The drums begin to roll, my boys, etc.

We aren't no thin red 'eroes, nor we aren't no
   blackguards too,
But single men in barricks, most remarkable like
   you;
An' if sometimes our conduck isn't all your
   fancy paints,
Why, single men in barricks don't grow into
   plaster saints.
   While it's Tommy this, an' Tommy that,
      an' "Tommy fall be'ind;"
   But it's "Please to walk in front, sir,"
      when there's trouble in the wind,
   There's trouble in the wind, my boys,
      etc.

You talk o' better food for us, an' schools, an'
    fires, an' all:

We'll wait for extry rations if you treat us
    rational.

Don't mess about the cook-room slops, but prove
    it to our face

The Widow's uniform is not the soldier-man's
    disgrace.

    For it's Tommy this, an' Tommy that,
        an' "Chuck him out, the brute!"

    But it's "Saviour of 'is country" when
        the guns begin to shoot;

    An' it's Tommy this, an' Tommy that,
        an' anything you please;

    An' Tommy ain't a bloomin' fool — you
        bet that Tommy sees!

" FUZZY WUZZY."

(Soudan Expeditionary Force.)

WE'VE fought with many men acrost the seas,
 An' some of 'em was brave an' some was not:
The Paythan an' the Zulu an' Burmese;
 But the Fuzzy was the finest o' the lot.
We never got a ha'porth's change of 'im:
 'E squatted in the scrub an' 'ocked our 'orses,
'E cut our sentries up at Sua*kim*,
 An' 'e played the cat an' banjo with our forces.
  So 'ere's *to* you, Fuzzy-Wuzzy, at your
   'ome in the Sowdan;
  You're a pore benighted 'eathen but a
   first-class fightin' man;
  We gives you your certifikit, an' if you
   want it signed
  We'll come an' 'ave a romp with you
   whenever you're inclined.

We took our chanst among the Kyber 'ills,
 The Boers knocked us silly at a mile,
The Burman guv us Irriwaddy chills,
 An' a Zulu *impi* dished us up in style:
But all we ever got from such as they
 Was pop to what the Fuzzy made us swaller;
We 'eld our bloomin' own, the papers say,
 But man for man the Fuzzy knocked us
    'oller.
    Then 'ere's *to* you, Fuzzy-Wuzzy, an' the
       missis and the kid;
    Our orders was to break you, an' of course
       we went an' did.
    We sloshed you with Martinis, an' it
       wasn't 'ardly fair;
    But for all the odds agin you, Fuzzy-Wuz,
       you bruk the square.

'E 'asn't got no papers of 'is own,
 'E 'asn't got no medals nor rewards,

So we must certify the skill 'e's shown
  In usin' of 'is long two-'anded swords:
When 'e's 'oppin' in an' out among the bush
  With 'is coffin-'eaded shield an' shovel-spear,
A 'appy day with Fuzzy on the rush
  Will last a 'ealthy Tommy for a year.
      So 'ere's *to* you, Fuzzy-Wuzzy, an' your
        friends which is no more,
      If we 'adn't lost some messmates we
        would 'elp you to deplore;
      But give an' take's the gospel, an' we'll
        call the bargain fair,
      For if you 'ave lost more than us, you
        crumpled up the square!

'E rushes at the smoke when we let drive,
  An', before we know, 'e's 'ackin' at our
    'ead;
'E's all 'ot sand an' ginger when alive,
  An' 'e's generally shammin' when 'e's dead.

'E's a daisy, 'e's a ducky, 'e's a lamb!
  'E's a injia-rubber idiot on the spree,
'E's the on'y thing that doesn't care a damn
  For the Regiment o' British Infantree.
      So 'ere's *to* you, Fuzzy-Wuzzy, at your
        'ome in the Sowdan;
      You're a pore benighted 'eathen but a
        first-class fightin' man;
      An' 'ere's *to* you, Fuzzy-Wuzzy, with your
        'ayrick 'ead of 'air —
      You big black boundin' beggar — for you
        bruk a British square.

OONTS !

(Northern India Transport Train.)

WOT makes the soldier's 'eart to penk, wot makes 'im to perspire ?

It isn't standin' up to charge or lyin' down to fire ;

But it's everlastin' waitin' on a everlastin' road

For the commissariat camel an' 'is commissariat load.

 O the *oont*,[1] O the *oont*, O the commissariat *oont !*

 With 'is silly neck a-bobbin' like a basket full o' snakes ;

 We packs 'im like a idol, an' you ought to 'ear 'im grunt,

 An' when we gets 'im loaded up 'is blessed girth-rope breaks.

---

[1] Camel· *oo* is pronounced like *u* in "bull," but by Mr. Atkins to rhyme with "front."

Wot makes the rear-guard swear so 'ard when
    night is drorin' in,
An' every native follower is shiverin' for 'is skin?
It ain't the chanst o' bein' rushed by Paythans
    frum the 'ills,
It's the commissariat camel puttin' on 'is blessed
    frills!
      O the *oont*, O the *oont*, O the hairy scary
      oont!
      A-trippin' over tent-ropes when we've got
      the night alarm;
      We socks 'im with a stretcher-pole an'
      'eads 'im off in front,
      An' when we've saved 'is bloomin' life 'e
      chaws our bloomin' arm.

The 'orse 'e knows above a bit, the bullock's but
    a fool,
The elephant's a gentleman, the baggage-mule's
    a mule;

But the commissariat cam - u - el, when all is said
    an' done,
'E's a devil an' a ostrich an' a orphan - child in one.
    O the *oont*, O the *oont*, O the Gawd - forsaken
        oont !
    The 'umpy - lumpy 'ummin' - bird a - singin'
        where 'e lies,
    'E's blocked the 'ole division from the
        rear - guard to the front,
    An' when we gets 'im up again — the
        beggar goes an' dies !

'E'll gall an' chafe an' lame an' fight; 'e smells
    most awful vile;
'E'll lose 'imself forever if you let 'im stray a
    mile;
'E's game to graze the 'ole day long an' 'owl the
    'ole night through,
An' when 'e comes to greasy ground 'e splits
    'isself in two.

O the *oont*, O the *oont*, O the floppin',
   droppin' *oont !*
When 'is long legs give from under an'
   'is meltin' eye is dim,
The tribes is up be'ind us an' the tribes
   is out in front,
It ain't no jam for Tommy, but it's kites
   and crows for 'im.

So when the cruel march is done an' when the
   roads is blind,
An' when we sees the camp in front an' 'ears
   the shots be'ind,
O then we strips 'is saddle off, and all 'is woes
   is past:
'E thinks on us that used 'im so, an' gets
   revenge at last.
      O the *oont*, O the *oont*, O the floatin',
         bloatin' *oont !*
      The late lamented camel in the water-cut
         he lies;

We keeps a mile behind 'im an' we keeps
  a mile in front,
But 'e gets into the drinkin' casks, and
  then o' course we dies.

LOOT.

IF you've ever stole a pheasant-egg be'ind the
    keeper's back,
  If you've ever snigged the washin' frum the line,
If you've ever crammed a gander in your bloomin'
    'aversack,
  You will understand this little song o' mine.
But the service rules are 'ard, an' frum such we
    are debarred,
  For the same with British morals does not
    suit (*Cornet:* Toot! toot!) —
W'y, they call a man a robber if 'e stuffs 'is
    marchin' clobber
With the —

(*Chorus.*) Loo! loo! Lulu! lulu! Loo! loo! Loot!
      loot! loot!
        'Ow the loot!
        Bloomin' loot!

That's the thing to make the boys git up
   an' shoot!
   It's the same with dogs an' men,
   If you'd make 'em come again
Clap 'em forward with a Loo! loo! Lulu!
   Loot!
(*ff*) Whoopee! Tear 'im, puppy! Loo! loo! Lulu!
   Loot! loot! loot!

If you've knocked a nigger edgeways when 'e's
   thrustin' for your life,
   You must leave 'im very careful where 'e
   fell;
An' may thank your stars an' gaiters if you
   didn't feel 'is knife
   That you ain't told off to bury him as
   well.
Then the sweatin' Tommies wonder as they spade
   the beggars under
Why lootin' should be entered as a crime;

So if my song you'll 'ear, I will learn you plain
    an' clear
  'Ow to pay yourself for fightin' overtime
    (*Chorus.*) With the loot, etc.

Now remember when you're 'acking round a gilded
    Burma god
  That 'is eyes is very often precious stones;
An' if you treat a nigger to a dose o' cleanin'-
    rod
  'E's like to show you everything 'e owns.
When 'e won't prodooce no more, pour some water
    on the floor
  Where you 'ear it answer 'ollow to the boot
    (*Cornet:* Toot! toot!) —
When the ground begins to sink, shove your
    baynick down the chink,
  An' you're sure to touch the —
(*Chorus.*) Loo! loo! Lulu! Loot! loot! loot!
        'Ow the loot, etc.

When from 'ouse to 'ouse you're 'untin' you must
    always work in pairs —
It 'alves the gain, but safer you will find —
For a single man gits bottled on them twisty-
    wisty stairs,
    An' a woman comes and clobs 'im from be'ind.
When you've turned 'em inside out, an' it seems
    beyond a doubt
    As if there weren't enough to dust a flute
    (*Cornet:* Toot! toot!) —
Before you sling your 'ook, at the 'ouse-tops
    take a look,
    For it's underneath the tiles they 'ide the loot.
    (*Chorus.*) 'Ow the loot, etc.

You can mostly square a Sergint an' a Quarter-
    master too,
    If you only take the proper way to go;
I could never keep my pickin's, but I've learned
    you all I knew —

An' don't you never say I told you so.

An' now I'll bid good-by, for I'm gettin' rather
dry,

An' I see another tunin' up to toot (*Cornet:*
Toot! toot!) —

So 'ere's good-luck to those that wears the
Widow's clo'es,

An' the Devil send 'em all they want o' loot!
(*Chorus.*) Yes, the loot,
Bloomin' loot.

In the tunic an' the mess-tin an' the boot!
It's the same with dogs an' men,
If you'd make 'em come again
Whoop 'em forward with the Loo! loo! Lulu!
Loot! loot! loot!

Heeya! Sick 'im, puppy! Loo! loo! Lulu!
Loot! loot! loot!

SOLDIER, SOLDIER.

"SOLDIER, soldier come from the wars,
　　Why don't you march with my true love?"
"We're fresh from off the ship, an' 'e's maybe
　　give the slip,
　An' you'd best go look for a new love."
　　　New love!　True love!
　　　Best go look for a new love,
　　　The dead they cannot rise, an' you'd better
　　　　　dry your eyes,
　　　An' you'd best go look for a new love.

"Soldier, soldier come from the wars,
　　What did you see o' my true love?"
"I see 'im serve the Queen in a suit o' rifle-
　　green,
　An' you'd best go look for a new love."

"Soldier, soldier come from the wars,

    Did ye see no more o' my true love?"

"I see 'im runnin' by when the shots begun

    to fly —

    But you'd best go look for a new love."

"Soldier, soldier come from the wars,

    Did aught take 'arm to my true love?"

"I couldn't see the fight, for the smoke it lay

    so white —

    An' you'd best go look for a new love."

"Soldier, soldier come from the wars,

    I'll up an' tend to my true love!"

"'E's lying on the dead with a bullet through

    'is 'ead,

    An' you'd best go look for a new love."

"Soldier, soldier come from the wars,

    I'll lie down an' die with my true love!"

"The pit we dug'll 'ide 'im an' twenty men
    beside 'im —
An' you'd best go look for a new love."

"Soldier, soldier come from the wars,
    Do you bring no sign from my true love?"
"I bring a lock of 'air that 'e allus used to
    wear,
    An' you'd best go look for a new love."

"Soldier, soldier come from the wars,
    O then I know it's true I've lost my true love!"
"An' I tell you truth again — when you've lost
    the feel o' pain
    You'd best take me for your true love."
        True love! New love!
        Best take 'im for a new love.
        The dead they cannot rise, an' you'd better
            dry your eyes,
        An' you'd best take 'im for your true love.

THE SONS OF THE WIDOW.

'AVE you 'eard o' the Widow at Windsor
 With a hairy gold crown on 'er 'ead?
She 'as ships on the foam — she 'as millions at 'ome,
 An' she pays us poor beggars in red.
  (Ow, poor beggars in red!)
There's 'er nick on the cavalry 'orses
 There's 'er mark on the medical stores —
An' 'er troopers you'll find with a fair wind be'ind
 That takes us to various wars.
  (Poor beggars! — barbarious wars!)
   Then 'ere's to the Widow at Windsor,
    An' 'ere's to the stores an' the guns,
   The men an' the 'orses what makes
    up the forces
   O' Missis Victorier's sons.
  (Poor beggars! — Victorier's sons!)

Walk wide o' the Widow at Windsor,

  For 'alf o' creation she owns:

We 'ave bought 'er the same with the sword
an' the flame,

  An' we've salted it down with our bones.

    (Poor beggars! — it's blue with our bones!)

Hands off o' the sons of the Widow,

  Hands off o' the goods in 'er shop,

For the Kings must come down an' the Emperors
frown

  When the Widow at Windsor says "Stop!"

    (Poor beggars! — we're sent to say "Stop!")

      Then 'ere's to the Lodge o' the Widow,

        From the Pole to the Tropics it
runs —

        To the Lodge that we tile with the
rank an' the file,

        An' open in forms with the guns.

    (Poor beggars! — it's always them guns!)

We 'ave 'eard o' the Widow at Windsor
  It's safest to let 'er alone:
For 'er sentries we stand by the sea an' the land
  Wherever the bugles are blown.
      (Poor beggars!—an' don't we get blown!)
Take 'old o' the wings o' the mornin',
  An' flop round the earth till you're dead;
But you won't get away from the tune that they
    play
  To. the bloomin' old rag over'ead.
      (Poor beggars!—it's 'ot over'ead!)
        Then 'ere's to the sons o' the Widow,
        Wherever, 'owever they roam.
        'Ere's all they desire, an' if they
          require
        A speedy return to their 'ome.
    (Poor beggars!—they'll never see 'ome!)

TROOPIN'.

(*Our Army in the East.*)

TROOPIN', troopin', troopin' to the sea:
  'Ere's September come again — the six-year
  men are free.
O leave the dead be'ind us, for they cannot
  come away
To where the ship's a-coalin' up that takes us
  'ome to-day.

    We're goin' 'ome, we're goin' 'ome,
    Our ship is *at* the shore,
    An' you must pack your 'aversack,
    For we won't come back no more.
    Ho, don't you grieve for me,
    My lovely Mary-Anne,
    For I'll marry you yit on a fourp'ny bit
    As a time-expired man.

The *Malabar'* in 'arbor with the *Jumner* at 'er
tail,

An' the time-expired's waitin' of 'is orders for to
sail.

O the weary waitin' when on Khyber 'ills we lay,

But the time-expired's waitin' of 'is orders
'ome to-day.

They'll turn us out at Portsmouth wharf in cold
an' wet an' rain,

All wearin' Injian cotton kit, but we will not
complain;

They'll kill us of pneumonia — for that's their
little way —

But damn the chills and fever, men, we're goin'
'ome to-day!

Troopin', troopin' — winter's round again!

See the new draf's pourin' in for the old
campaign;

Ho, you poor recruities, but you've got to earn
    your pay—
What's the last from Lunnon, lads? We're goin'
    there to-day.

Troopin', troopin', give another cheer—
'Ere's to English women an' a quart of English
    beer;
The Colonel an' the regiment an' all who've got
    to stay,
Gawd's mercy strike 'em gentle—Whoop! we're
    goin' 'ome to-day.
      We're goin' 'ome, we're goin' 'ome,
      Our ship is *at* the shore,
      An' you must pack your 'aversack,
      For we won't come back no more.
      Ho, don't you grieve for me,
      My lovely Mary-Anne,
      For I'll marry you yit on a fourp'ny bit
      As a time-expired man.

GUNGA DIN.

THE *bhisti,* or water-carrier, attached to regiments in India, is often one of the most devoted of the Queen's servants. He is also appreciated by the men.

[THIS BALLAD IS EXTENSIVELY PLAGIARIZED.]

YOU may talk o' gin an' beer
      When you're quartered safe out 'ere,
An' you're sent to penny - fights an' Aldershot it;
But if it comes to slaughter
You will do your work on water,
An' you'll lick the bloomin' boots of 'im that's
      got it.
Now in Injia's sunny clime,
Where I used to spend my time
A - servin' of 'Er Majesty the Queen,
Of all them black - faced crew
The finest man I knew
Was our regimental *bhisti,* Gunga Din.

He was "Din! Din! Din!

You limping lump o' brick-dust, Gunga
    Din!

Hi! *slippy hitherao!*

Water, get it! *Panee lao!*[1]

You squidgy-nosed old idol, Gunga Din!"

The uniform 'e wore

Was nothin' much before,

An' rather less than 'arf o' that be'ind,

For a twisty piece o' rag

An' a goatskin water-bag

Was all the field-equipment 'e could find.

When the sweatin' troop-train lay

In a sidin' through the day,

Where the 'eat would make your bloomin' eye-
    brows crawl,

We shouted "Harry By!"[2]

---

[1] Bring water swiftly.
[2] Mr. Atkins's equivalent for "O Brother!"

Till our throats were bricky-dry,

Then we wopped 'im 'cause 'e couldn't serve
  us all.

  It was "Din! Din! Din!

  You 'eathen, where the mischief 'ave you
    been?

  You put some *juldee* in it,

  Or I'll *marrow* you this minute[1]

  If you don't fill up my helmet, Gunga
    Din!"

'E would dot an' carry one

Till the longest day was done,

An' 'e didn't seem to know the use o' fear.

If we charged or broke or cut,

You could bet your bloomin' nut,

'E'd be waitin' fifty paces right flank rear.

With 'is *mussick* on 'is back,

'E would skip with our attack,

An' watch us till the bugles made "Retire."

[1] Hit you.

An' for all 'is dirty 'ide
'E was white, clear white, inside
When 'e went to tend the wounded under fire!
    It was "Din! Din! Din!"
    With the bullets kickin' dust-spots on the
        green.
    When the cartridges ran out,
    You could 'ear the front-files shout:
    "Hi! ammunition-mules an' Gunga Din!"

I sha'n't forgit the night
When I dropped be'ind the fight
With a bullet where my belt-plate should 'a'
    been.
I was chokin' mad with thirst,
An' the man that spied me first
Was our good old grinnin', gruntin' Gunga Din.
'E lifted up my 'ead,
An' 'e plugged me where I bled,
An' 'e guv me 'arf-a-pint o' water—green:

It was crawlin' and it stunk,

But of all the drinks I've drunk,

I'm gratefullest to one from Gunga Din.

> It was "Din! Din! Din!
>
> 'Ere's a beggar with a bullet through 'is
> spleen;
>
> 'E's chawin' up the ground an' 'e's kickin'
> all around:
>
> For Gawd's sake git the water, Gunga
> Din!"

'E carried me away

To where a *dooli* lay,

An' a bullet come an' drilled the beggar clean.

'E put me safe inside,

An' just before 'e died:

"I 'ope you liked your drink," sez Gunga Din.

So I'll meet 'im later on

In the place where 'e is gone —

Where it's always double drill and no canteen;

'E'll be squattin' on the coals

Givin' drink to pore damned souls,

An' I'll get a swig in Hell from Gunga Din!

 Din! Din! Din!

 You Lazarushian - leather Gunga Din!

 Tho' I've belted you an' flayed you,

 By the livin' Gawd that made you,

 You're a better man than I am, Gunga

  Din!

MANDALAY.

BY the old Moulmein Pagoda, lookin' eastward
    to the sea,
There's a Burma girl a-settin', an' I know she
    thinks o' me;
For the wind is in the palm-trees, an' the
    temple-bells they say:
"Come you back, you British soldier; come you
    back to Mandalay!"
      Come you back to Mandalay,
      Where the old Flotilla lay:
      Can't you 'ear their paddles chunkin' from
          Rangoon to Mandalay?
      O the road to Mandalay,
      Where the flyin'-fishes play,
      An' the dawn comes up like thunder outer
          China 'crost the Bay!

'Er petticut was yaller an' 'er little cap was
    green,

An' 'er name was Supi-yaw-lat — jes' the same
    as Theebaw's Queen,

An' I seed her fust a-smokin' of a whackin'
    white cheroot,

An' a-wastin' Christian kisses on an 'eathen
    idol's foot:

    Bloomin' idol made o' mud —

    Wot they called the Great Gawd Budd —

    Plucky lot she cared for idols when I

        kissed 'er where she stud !

    On the road to Mandalay —

When the mist was on the rice-fields an' the
    sun was droppin' slow,

She'd git 'er little banjo an' she'd sing "*Kulla-
lo-lo !*"

With 'er arm upon my shoulder an' her cheek
    agin my cheek

We useter watch the steamers an' the *hathis*
    pilin' teak.

 Elephints a-pilin' teak
 In the sludgy, squdgy creek,
 Where the silence 'ung that 'eavy you was
  'arf afraid to speak!
 On the road to Mandalay —

But that's all shove be'ind me — long ago an'
    fur away,
An' there ain't no 'buses runnin' from the Benk
    to Mandalay;
An' I'm learnin' 'ere in London what the ten-
    year sodger tells:
"If you've 'eard the East a-callin', why, you
    won't 'eed nothin' else."

 No! you won't 'eed nothin' else
 But them spicy garlic smells
 An' the sunshine an' the palm-trees an'
  the tinkly temple-bells!
 On the road to Mandalay —

I am sick o' wastin' leather on these gutty
  pavin'-stones,
An' the blasted Henglish drizzle wakes the fever
  in my bones;
Tho' I walks with fifty 'ousemaids outer Chelsea
  to the Strand,
An' they talks a lot o' lovin', but wot do they
  understand?

  Beefy face an' grubby 'and —
  Law! wot *do* they understand?
  I've a neater, sweeter maiden in a cleaner,
    greener land!
  On the road to Mandalay —

Ship me somewheres east of . Suez where the
  best is like the worst,
Where there aren't no Ten Commandments, an' a
  man can raise a thirst;
For the temple-bells are callin', an' it's there
  that I would be —

By the old Moulmein Pagoda, lookin' lazy at
the sea —

On the road to Mandalay,

Where the old Flotilla lay,

With our sick beneath the awnings when
we went to Mandalay!

Oh, the road to Mandalay,

Where the flyin'-fishes play,

An' the dawn comes up like thunder outer
China 'crost the Bay!

THE YOUNG BRITISH SOLDIER.

WHEN the 'arf-made recruity goes out to the
    East
'E acts like a babe an' 'e drinks like a beast,
An' 'e wonders because 'e is frequent deceased
    Ere 'e's fit for to serve as a soldier.
      Serve, serve, serve as a soldier,
      Serve, serve, serve as a soldier,
      Serve, serve, serve as a soldier,
        So-oldier *hof* the Queen!

Now all you recruities what's drafted tc-day,
You shut up your rag-box an' 'ark to my lay,
An' I'll sing you a soldier as far as I may:
    A soldier what's fit for a soldier.
      Fit, fit, fit for a soldier—

First, mind you steer clear o' the grog-sellers' huts,
For they sell you Fixed Bay'nets that rots out
    your guts —
Ay, drink that 'ud eat the live steel from your
    butts —
        An' it's bad for the young British soldier.
          Bad, bad, bad for the soldier —

When the cholera comes — as it will past a doubt —
Keep out of the wet and don't go on the shout,
For the sickness comes in as the liquor dies out,
        An' it crumples the young British soldier.
          Crum-, crum-, crumples the soldier —

But the worst o' your foes is the sun over'ead;
You *must* wear your 'elmet for all that is said.
If 'e finds you uncovered 'e'll knock you down
    dead,
        An' you'll die like a fool of a soldier.
          Fool, fool, fool of a soldier —

If you're cast for fatigue by a sergeant unkind,
Don't grouse like a woman nor crack on nor blind;
Be handy and civil, and then you will find
> As it's beer for the young British soldier.
> Beer, beer, beer for the soldier —

Now, if you must marry, take care she is old —
A troop-sergeant's widow's the nicest I'm told —
For beauty won't help if your vittles is cold,
> An' love ain't enough for a soldier.
> 'Nough, 'nough, 'nough for a soldier —

If the wife should go wrong with a comrade, be loath
To shoot when you catch 'em — you'll swing, on my oath! —
Make 'im take 'er and keep 'er; that's hell for them both,
> An' you're quit o' the curse of a soldier.
> Curse, curse, curse of a soldier —

When first under fire an' you're wishful to duck,
Don't look or take 'eed at the man that is
    struck,
Be thankful you're livin' an' trust to your luck,
    An' march to your front like a soldier.˙
      Front, front, front like a soldier.

When 'arf of your bullets fly wide in the ditch,
Don't call your Martini a cross-eyed old bitch;
She's human as you are — you treat her as sich,
    An' she'll fight for the young British sol-
      dier.
      Fight, fight, fight for the soldier —

When shakin' their bustles like ladies so fine
The guns o' the enemy wheel into line;
Shoot low at the limbers and don't mind the
    shine,
    For noise never startles the soldier.
      Start-, start-, startles the soldier —

If your officer's dead and the sergeants look white,
Remember it's ruin to run from a fight;
So take open order, lie down, and sit tight,
 An' wait for supports like a soldier.
  Wait, wait, wait like a soldier —

When you're wounded an' left on Afghanistan's
 plains,
An' the women come out to cut up your re-
 mains,
Jest roll to your rifle an' blow out your brains,
 An' go to your Gawd like a soldier:
  Go, go, go like a soldier,
  Go, go, go like a soldier,
  Go, go, go like a soldier,
   So-oldier *hof* the Queen.

SCREW-GUNS.

SMOKIN' my pipe on the mountings, sniffin'
the mornin'-cool,
I walks in my old brown gaiters along o' my
old brown mule,
With seventy gunners be'ind me, an' never a
beggar forgets
It's only the pick o' the Army that handles the
dear little pets — Tss! Tss!

For you all love the screw-guns — the screw-
guns they all love you.
So when we call round with a few guns, o' course
you will know what to do — hoo! hoo!
Jest send in your Chief an' surrender — it's
worse if you fights or you runs:
You can go where you please, you can skid
up the trees, but you don't get away from
the guns.

They send us along where the roads are, but
　　mostly we goes where they ain't;
We'd climb up the side of a sign-board an'
　　trust to the stick o' the paint;
We've chivied the Naga an' Lushai, we've give
　　the Afreedeeman fits,
For we fancies ourselves at two thousand, we
　　guns that are built in two bits — Tss! Tss!
　　　For you all love the screw-guns —

If a man doesn't work, why, we drills 'im an'
　　teaches 'im 'ow to be'ave;
If a beggar can't march, why, we kills 'im an'
　　rattles 'im into 'is grave.
You've got to stand up to our business an'
　　spring without snatchin' or fuss.
D' you say that you sweat with the field-guns?
　　By God, you must lather with us — Tss!
Tss !
　　　For you all love the screw-guns —

The eagles is screamin' around us, the river's
    a-moanin' below,
We're clear o' the pine an' the oak-scrub, we're
    out on the rocks an' the snow,
An' the wind is as thin as a whip-lash what
    carries away to the plains
The rattle an' stamp o' the lead-mules — the
    jinglety-jink o' the chains — Tss! Tss!
      For you all love the screw-guns —

There's a wheel on the Horns o' the Mornin'
    an' a wheel on the edge o' the Pit,
An' a drop into nothin' beneath us as straight
    as a beggar can spit;
With the sweat runnin' out o' your shirt-
    sleeves an' the sun off the snow in your
    face,
An' 'arf o' the men on the drag-ropes to hold
    the old gun in 'er place — Tss! Tss!
      For you all love the screw-guns —

Smokin' my pipe on the mountings, sniffin' the mornin'-cool,

I climbs in my old brown gaiters along o' my old brown mule.

The monkey can say what our road was — the wild-goat 'e knows where we passed.

Stand easy, you long-eared old darlin's! Out drag-ropes! With shrapnel! Hold fast! — Tss! Tss!

    For you all love the screw-guns — the screw-guns they all love you!

    So when we take tea with a few guns, o' course you will know what to do — hoo! hoo!

    Just send in your Chief and surrender — it's worse if you fights or you runs:

    You may hide in the caves, they'll be only your graves, but you don't get away from the guns!

BELTS.

THERE was a row in Silver Street that's near
   to Dublin Quay,
Between an Irish regiment an' English cavalree;
It started at Revelly an' it lasted on till dark;
The first man dropped at Harrison's, the last
   forninst the Park.
     For it was "Belts, belts, belts, an' that's
       one for you!"
     An' it was "Belts, belts, belts, an' that's
       done for you!"
     O buckle an' tongue
     Was the song that we sung
     From Harrison's on to the Park!

There was a row in Silver Street—the regiments
   was out,
They called us "Delhi Rebels," an' we answered
   "Threes about!"

That drew them like a hornet's nest — we met
    them good an' large,
The English at the double an' the Irish at the
    charge.
      Then it was: Belts —

There was a row in Silver Street — an' I was in
    it too;
We passed the time o' day, an' then the belts
    went *whirraru;*
I misremember what occurred, but subsequint the
    storm
A *Freeman's Journal Supplemint* was all my
    uniform.
      O it was: Belts —

There was a row in Silver Street — they sent the
    Polis there,
The English were too drunk to know, the Irish
    didn't care;

But when they grew impertinint we simultaneous
  rose,

Till half o' them was Liffey mud an' half was
  tatthered clo'es.

    For it was: Belts —

There was a row in Silver Street — it might ha'
  raged till now,

But some one drew his side-arm clear, an'
  nobody knew how;

'Twas Hogan took the point an' dropped; we
  saw the red blood run:

An' so we all was murderers that started out in
  fun.

    While it was: Belts —

There was a row in Silver Street — but that took
  off the shine,

Wid each man whishperin' to his next: "'Twas
  never work o' mine!"

We went away like beaten dogs, an' down the
    street we bore him,
The poor dumb corpse that couldn't see the
    bhoys were sorry for him.
      When it was: Belts —

There was a row in Silver Street — it isn't over
    yet,
For half of us are under guard wid punishmints
    to get;
'Tis all a mericle to me as in the Clink I lie;
There was a row in Silver Street — begod, I
    wonder why!
      But it was "Belts, belts, belts, an' that's
        one for you!"
      An' it was "Belts, belts, belts, an' that's
        done for you!"
      O buckle an' tongue
      Was the song that we sung
      From Harrison's down to the Park!

TO THE UNKNOWN GODDESS.

WILL you conquer my heart with your beauty;
    my soul going out from afar?
Shall I fall to your hand as a victim of crafty
    and cautious *shikar?*

Have I met you and passed you already,
    unknowing, unthinking and blind?
Shall I meet you next session at Simla, O
    sweetest and best of your kind?

Does the P. and O. bear you to me-ward, or,
    clad in short frocks in the West,
Are you growing the charms that shall capture
    and torture the heart in my breast?

113

Will you stay in the Plains till September — my
    passion as warm as the day?
Will you bring me to book on the Mountains,
    or where the thermantidotes play?

When the light of your eyes shall make pallid
    the mean lesser lights I pursue,
And the charm of your presence shall lure me
    from love of the gay "thirteen-two;"

When the peg and the pig-skin shall please not;
    when I buy me Calcutta-built clothes;
When I quit the Delight of Wild Asses; for-
    swearing the swearing of oaths;

As a deer to the hand of the hunter when I
    turn 'mid the gibes of my friends;
When the days of my freedom are numbered,
    and the life of the bachelor ends.

Ah Goddess! child, spinster, or widow — as of
 old on Mars Hill when they raised
To the God that they knew not an altar — so
 I, a young Pagan, have praised

The Goddess I know not nor worship; yet, if
 half that men tell me be true,
You will come in the future, and therefore these
 verses are written to you.

THE RUPAIYAT OF OMAR KAL'VIN.

[ALLOWING for the difference 'twixt prose and rhymed exaggeration, this ought to reproduce the sense of what Sir A—— told the nation some time ago, when the Government struck from our incomes two per cent.]

NOW the New Year, reviving last Year's Debt,
The Thoughtful Fisher casteth wide his Net;
So I with begging Dish and ready Tongue
Assail all Men for all that I can get.

Imports indeed are gone with all their Dues —
Lo! Salt a Lever that I dare not use,
Nor may I ask the Tillers in Bengal —
Surely my Kith and Kin will not refuse!

Pay — and I promise by the Dust of Spring,
Retrenchment. If my promises can bring
Comfort, Ye have Them now a thousand-fold —
By Allah! I will promise *Anything!*

Indeed, indeed, Retrenchment oft before
I swore — but did I mean it when I swore?
  And then, and then, We wandered to the Hills,
And so the Little Less became Much More.

Whether at Boileaugunge or Babylon,
I know not how the wretched Thing is done,
  The Items of Receipt grow surely small;
The Items of Expense mount one by one.

I cannot help it. What have I to do
With One and Five, or Four, or Three, or Two?
  Let Scribes spit Blood and Sulphur as they
    please,
Or Statemen call me foolish — Heed not you.

Behold, I promise — Anything You will.
Behold, I greet you with an empty Till —
  Ah! Fellow-Sinners, of your Charity
Seek not the Reason of the Dearth, but fill.

For if I sinned and fell, where lies the Gain
Of Knowledge? Would it ease you of your
    Pain
  To know the tangled Threads of Revenue,
I ravel deeper in a hopeless Skein?

"Who hath not Prudence"—what was it I said,
Of Her who paints her Eyes and tires Her
    Head,
  And gibes and mocks the People in the Street,
And fawns upon them for Her thriftless Bread?

Accursed is She of Eve's daughters—She
Hath cast off Prudence, and Her End shall be
  Destruction . . . Brethren, of your Bounty
    grant
Some portion of your daily Bread to *Me*.

LA NUIT BLANCHE.

A MUCH-DISCERNING Public hold
  The Singer generally sings
  Of personal and private things,
And prints and sells his past for gold.

Whatever I may here disclaim,
  The very clever folk I sing to
  Will most indubitably cling to
Their pet delusion, just the same.

I HAD seen, as dawn was breaking
  And I staggered to my rest,
Tarı Devi softly shaking
  From the Cart Road to the crest.
I had seen the spurs of Jakko
  Heave and quiver, swell and sink.
Was it Earthquake or tobacco,
  Day of Doom or Night of Drink?

In the full, fresh, fragrant morning
  I observed a camel crawl,

Laws of gravitation scorning,
　On the ceiling and the wall;
Then I watched a fender walking,
　And I heard gray leeches sing,
And a red-hot monkey talking
　Did not seem the proper thing.

Then a Creature, skinned and crimson,
　Ran about the floor and cried,
And they said I had the "jims" on,
　And they dosed me with bromide,
And they locked me in my bedroom —
　Me and one wee Blood Red Mouse —
Though I said: "To give my head room
　"You had best unroof the house."

But my words were all unheeded,
　Though I told the grave M.D.
That the treatment really needed
　Was a dip in open sea

That was lapping just below me,
  Smooth as silver, white as snow,
And it took three men to throw me
  When I found I could not go.

Half the night I watched the Heavens
  Fizz like '81 champagne —
Fly to sixes and to sevens,
  Wheel and thunder back again;
And when all was peace and order
  Save one planet nailed askew,
Much I wept because my warder
  Would not let me set it true.

After frenzied hours of waiting,
  When the Earth and Skies were dumb,
Pealed an awful voice dictating
  An interminable sum,
Changing to a tangled story —
  "What she said you said I said —"

Till the Moon arose in glory,
  And I found her . . . in my head;

Then a Face came, blind and weeping,
  And It couldn't wipe Its eyes,
And It muttered I was keeping
  Back the moonlight from the skies;
So I patted It for pity,
  But It whistled shrill with wrath,
And a huge black Devil City
  Poured its peoples on my path.

So I fled with steps uncertain
  On a thousand-year long race,
But the bellying of the curtain
  Kept me always in one place;
While the tumult rose and maddened
  To the roar of Earth on fire,
Ere it ebbed and sank and saddened
  To a whisper tense as wire.

In intolerable stillness
  Rose one little, little star,
And it chuckled at my illness,
  And it mocked me from afar;
And its brethren came and eyed me,
  Called the Universe to aid,
Till I lay, with naught to hide me,
  'Neath the Scorn of All Things Made.

Dun and saffron, robed and splendid,
  Broke the solemn, pitying Day,
And I knew my pains were ended,
  And I turned and tried to pray;
But my speech was shattered wholly,
  And I wept as children weep,
Till the dawn-wind, softly, slowly,
  Brought to burning eyelids sleep.

MY RIVAL.

I GO to concert, party, ball —
   What profit is in these?
I sit alone against the wall
   And strive to look at ease.
The incense that is mine by right
   They burn before Her shrine;
And that's because I'm seventeen
   And She is forty - nine.

I cannot check my girlish blush,
   My color comes and goes;
I redden to my finger - tips,
   And sometimes to my nose.
But She is white where white should be,
   And red where red should shine.

The blush that flies at seventeen
  Is fixed at forty - nine.

I wish *I* had Her constant cheek:
  I wish that I could sing
All sorts of funny little songs,
  Not quite the proper thing.
I'm very *gauche* and very shy,
  Her jokes aren't in my line;
  And, worst of all, I'm seventeen
  While She is forty - nine.

The young men come, the young men go,
  Each pink and white and neat,
She's older than their mothers, but
  They grovel at Her feet.
They walk beside Her *'rickshaw* wheels —
  None ever walk by mine;
And that's because I'm seventeen
  And She is forty - nine.

She rides with half a dozen men,
   (She calls them "boys" and "mashers")
I trot along the Mall alone;
   My prettiest frocks and sashes
Don't help to fill my programme-card,
   And vainly I repine
From ten to two A.M. Ah me!
   Would I were forty-nine!

She calls me "darling," "pet," and "dear,"
   And "sweet retiring maid."
I'm always at the back, I know,
   She puts me in the shade.
She introduces me to men,
   "Cast" lovers, I opine,
For sixty takes to seventeen,
   Nineteen to forty-nine.

But even She must older grow
   And end Her dancing days,

She can't go on forever so
  At concerts, balls, and plays.
One ray of priceless hope I see
  Before my footsteps shine;
Just think, that She'll be eighty - one
  When I am forty - nine.

THE LOVERS' LITANY.

EYES of gray — a sodden quay,
  Driving rain and falling tears,
As the steamer wears to sea
In a parting storm of cheers.
  Sing, for Faith and Hope are high —
  None so true as you and I —
  Sing the Lovers' Litany : —
  "Love like ours can never die!"

Eyes of black — a throbbing keel,
Milky foam to left and right;
Whispered converse near the wheel
In the brilliant tropic night.
  Cross that rules the Southern Sky!
  Stars that sweep and wheel and fly,
  Hear the Lovers' Litany : —
  "Love like ours can never die!"

Eyes of brown — a dusty plain
Split and parched with heat of June,
Flying hoof and tightened rein,
Hearts that beat the old, old tune.
 Side by side the horses fly,
 Frame we now the old reply
 Of the Lovers' Litany : —
 " Love like ours can never die ! "

Eyes of blue — the Simla Hills
Silvered with the moonlight hoar ;
Pleading of the waltz that thrills,
Dies and echoes round Benmore.
 " Mabel," " Officers," " Good - by,"
 Glamour, wine, and witchery —
 On my soul's sincerity,
 " Love like ours can never die ! "

Maidens, of your charity,
Pity my most luckless state.

Four times Cupid's debtor I—
Bankrupt in quadruplicate.

Yet, despite this evil case,
An a maiden showed me grace,
Four - and - forty times would I
Sing the Lovers' Litany : —
"Love like ours can never die!"

A BALLAD OF BURIAL.

("*Saint Praxed's ever was the Church for peace.*")

IF down here I chance to die,
  Solemnly I beg you take
All that is left of "I"
  To the Hills for old sake's sake.
Pack me very thoroughly
  In the ice that used to slake
Pegs I drank when I was dry —
  This observe for old sake's sake.

To the railway station hie,
  There a single ticket take
For Umballa — goods - train — I
  Shall not mind delay or shake.
I shall rest contentedly
  Spite of clamor coolies make;

Thus in state and dignity
  Send me up for old sake's sake.

Next the sleepy Babu wake,
  Book a Kalka van "for four."
Few, I think, will care to make
  Journeys with me any more
As they used to do of yore.
  I shall need a "special" break —
Thing I never took before —
  Get me one for old sake's sake.

After that — arrangements make.
  No hotel will take me in,
And a bullock's back would break
  'Neath the teak and leaden skin.
Tonga ropes are frail and thin,
  Or, did I a back - seat take,
In a tonga I might spin, —
  Do your best for old sake's sake.

After that — your work is done.
 Recollect a Padre must
Mourn the dear departed one —
 Throw the ashes and the dust.
Don't go down at once. I trust
 You will find excuse to "snake
Three days' casual on the bust,"
 Get your fun for old sake's sake.

I could never stand the Plains.
 Think of blazing June and May,
Think of those September rains
 Yearly till the Judgment Day!
I should never rest in peace,
 I should sweat and lie awake.
Rail me then, on my decease,
 To the Hills for old sake's sake.

DIVIDED DESTINIES.

IT was an artless *Bandar*, and he danced upon
  a pine,
And much I wondered how he lived, and where
  the beast might dine,
And many, many other things, till, o'er my
  morning smoke,
I slept the sleep of idleness and dreamt that
  Bandar spoke.

He said: "O man of many clothes! Sad
  crawler on the Hills!
Observe, I know not Ranken's shop, nor Ranken's monthly bills;
I take no heed to trousers or the coats that
  you call dress;
Nor am I plagued with little cards for little
  drinks at Mess.

"I steal the bunnia's grain at morn, at noon
  and eventide,
 (For he is fat and I am spare), I roam the
  mountain side,
 I follow no man's carriage, and no, never in
  my life
 Have I flirted at Peliti's with another *Bandar's*
  wife.

"O man of futile fopperies — unnecessary wraps;
 I own no ponies in the hills, I drive no tall-
  wheeled traps;
 I buy me not twelve - button gloves, 'short-
  sixes' eke, or rings,
 Nor do I waste at Hamilton's my wealth on
  'pretty things.'

"I quarrel with my wife at home, we never
  fight abroad;
 But Mrs. B. has grasped the fact I am her
  only lord.

I never heard of fever — dumps nor debts de-
press my soul;
And I pity and despise you!" Here he pouched
my breakfast-roll.

His hide was very mangy, and his face was very red,
And ever and anon he scratched with energy his
head.
His manners were not always nice, but how
my spirit cried
To be an artless *Bandar* loose upon the mountain
side!

So I answered: "Gentle *Bandar,* an inscrutable
Decree
Makes thee a gleesome fleasome Thou, and me a
wretched Me.
Go! Depart in peace, my brother, to thy home
amid the pine;
Yet forget not once a mortal wished to change
his lot with thine."

THE MASQUE OF PLENTY.

ARGUMENT. — The Indian Government, being minded to discover the economic condition of their lands, sent a Committee to inquire into it, and saw that it was good.

SCENE. — *The wooded heights of Simla. The Incarnation of the Government of India in the raiment of the Angel of Plenty sings, to pianoforte accompaniment :—*

"HOW sweet is the shepherd's sweet life!
　　From the dawn to the even he strays—
He shall follow his sheep all the day,
　　And his tongue shall be fillèd with praise.

　　(*Adagio dim.*) Fillèd with praise!"

(*Largendo con sp.*) Now this is the position,
　　　　　　　　Go make an inquisition
　　　　　　　　Into their real condition
　　　　　　　　As swiftly as ye may.

(*p.*) Ay, paint our swarthy billions
    The richest of vermilions
    Ere two well-led cotillions
    Have danced themselves away.

TURKISH PATROL, *as able and intelligent Investigators wind down the Himalayas:* —

What is the state of the Nation? What is its
    occupation?
Hi! get along, get along, get along — lend us
    the information!

(*Dim.*) Census the *byle* and the *yabu* — capture a
    first-class Babu,
Set him to cut Gazetteers — Gazetteers . . .
    (*ff.*) What is the state of the Nation, etc., etc.

INTERLUDE, *from Nowhere in Particular, to stringed
    and Oriental instruments.*

Our cattle reel beneath the yoke they bear —
    The earth is iron, and the skies are brass —

And faint with fervor of the flaming air
  The languid hours pass.

The well is dry beneath the village tree —
  The young wheat withers ere it reach a
    span,   .
And belts of blinding sand show cruelly
  Where once the river ran.

Pray, brothers, pray, but to no earthly King —
  Lift up your hands above the blighted grain,
Look westward — if they please, the Gods shall
    bring
  Their mercy with the rain.

Look westward — bears the blue no brown cloud-
    bank ?
  Nay, it is written — wherefore should we fly ?
On our own field and by our cattle's flank
    Lie down, lie down to die !

SEMI - CHORUS.

By the plumed heads of Kings
　　　　Waving high,
Where the tall corn springs
　　　　O'er the dead.

If they rust or rot we die,
If they ripen we are fed.
Very mighty is the power of our Kings!

Triumphal return to Simla of the Investigators,
attired after the manner of Dionysus, leading a
pet tiger-cub in wreaths of rhubarb leaves, sym-
bolical of India under medical treatment. They
sing:—

We have seen, we have written — behold it, the
　　proof of our manifold toil!
In their hosts they assembled and told it — the
　　tale of the sons of the soil.

We have said of the Sickness, "Where is it?"—
  and of Death, "It is far from our ken;"
We have paid a particular visit to the affluent
  children of men.
We have trodden the mart and the well-curb—
  we have stooped to the bield and the byre;
And the King may the forces of Hell curb, for
  the People have all they desire!

Castanets and step-dance:

Oh, the *dom* and the *mag* and the *thakur* and
  the *thag,*
      And the *nat* and the *brinjaree,*
And the *bunnia* and the *ryot* are as happy and
  as quiet
      And as plump as they can be!
Yes, the *jain* and the *jat* in his stucco-fronted hut,
      And the bounding *bazugar,*
By the favor of the King, are as fat as anything,
      They are—they are—they are!

RECITATIVE, *Government of India, with white satin wings and electroplated harp:* —

How beautiful upon the mountains — in peace reclining,

Thus to be assured that our people are unanimously dining.

And though there are places not so blessed as others in natural advantages, which, after all, was only to be expected,

Proud and glad are we to congratulate you upon the work you have thus ably effected.

(*Cres.*) How be‑ewtiful upon the mountains!

HIRED BAND, *brasses only, full chorus:* —

God bless the Squire
And all his rich relations
Who teach us poor people
We eat our proper rations —
We eat our proper rations,
In spite of inundations,

Malarial exhalations,

And casual starvations,

We have, we have, they say we have—

We *have* our proper rations!

(*Cornet.*)

Which nobody can deny!

If he does he tells a lie—

We are all as willing as Barkis—

We all of us loves the Markiss—

We all of us stuffs our ca-ar-kis—

With food until we die! (*Da capo*)

CHORUS OF THE CRYSTALLIZED FACTS.

Before the beginning of years

There came to the rule of the State

Men with a pair of shears,

Men with an Estimate—

Strachey with Muir for leaven,

Lytton with locks that fell,

Ripon fooling with Heaven,
And Temple riding like H–ll!
And the bigots took in hand
Cess and the falling of rain,
And the measure of sifted sand
The dealer puts in the grain —
Imports by land and sea,
To uttermost decimal worth,
And registration — free —
In the houses of death and of birth:
And fashioned with pens and paper,
And fashioned in black and white,
With Life for a flickering taper
And Death for a blazing light — .
With the Armed and the Civil Power,
That his strength might endure for a span,
From Adam's Bridge to Peshawur,
The Much Administered man.

In the towns of the North and the East,
They gathered as unto rule,

They bade him starve the priest
And send his children to school.
Railways and roads they wrought,
For the needs of the soil within;
A time to squabble in court,
A time to bear and to grin.
And gave him peace in his ways,
Jails — and Police to fight,
Justice at length of days,
And Right — and Might in the Right.
His speech is of mortgaged bedding,
On his kine he borrows yet,
At his heart is his daughter's wedding,
In his eye foreknowledge of debt.
He eats and hath indigestion,
He toils and he may not stop;
His life is a long-drawn question
Between a crop and a crop.

THE MARE'S NEST.

JANE Austen Beecher Stowe de Rouse
    Was good beyond all earthly need;
But, on the other ·hand, her spouse
    Was very, very bad indeed.
He smoked cigars, called churches slow,
    And raced — but this she did not know.

For Belial Machiavelli kept
    The little fact a secret, and,
Though o'er his minor sins she wept,
    Jane Austen did not understand
That Lilly — thirteen-two and bay —
Absorbed one half her husband's pay.

     ·

She was so good, she made him worse;
    (Some women are like this, I think;)

He taught her parrot how to curse,
  Her Assam monkey how to drink.
He vexed her righteous soul until
She went up, and he went down hill.

Then came the crisis, strange to say,
  Which turned a good wife to a better.
A telegraphic peon, one day,
  Brought her — now, had it been a letter
For Belial Machiavelli, I
Know Jane would just have let it lie.

But 'twas a telegram instead,
  Marked "urgent," and her duty plain
To open it. Jane Austen read: —
  "Your Lilly's got a cough again.
Can't understand why she is kept
At your expense." Jane Austin wept.

It was a misdirected wire.
  Her husband was at Shaitanpore.

She spread her anger, hot as fire,
    Through six thin foreign sheets or more,
Sent off that letter, wrote another
To her solicitor — and mother.

Then Belial Machiavelli saw
    Her error and, I trust, his own,
Wired to the minion of the Law,   ·
    And travelled wifeward — not alone.
For Lilly — thirteen-two and bay —
Came in a horse-box all the way.

There was a scene — a weep or two —
    With many kisses. Austen Jane
Rode Lilly all the season through,
    And never opened wires again.
She races now with Belial. This
Is very sad, but so it is.

POSSIBILITIES.

AY, lay him 'neath the Simla pine —
    A fortnight fully to be missed,
  Behold, we lose our fourth at whist,
A chair is vacant where we dine.

His place forgets him; other men
    Have bought his ponies, guns, and traps.
    His fortune is the Great Perhaps
And that cool rest-house down the glen,

Whence he shall hear, as spirits may,
    Our mundane revel on the height,
    Shall watch each flashing *'rickshaw*-light
Sweep on to dinner, dance, and play.

Benmore shall woo him to the ball
　　With lighted rooms and braying band,
　　And he shall hear and understand
"*Dream Faces*" better than us all.

For, think you, as the vapors flee
　　Across Sanjaolie after rain,
　　His soul may climb the hill again
To each old field of victory.

Unseen, who women held so dear,
　　The strong man's yearning to his kind
　　Shall shake at most the window - blind,
Or dull awhile the card - room's cheer.

In his own place of power unknown,
　　His Light o' Love another's flame,
　　His dearest pony galloped lame,
And he an alien and alone.

Yet may he meet with many a friend—
　　Shrewd shadows, lingering long unseen
　　Among us when "*God save the Queen*"
Shows even "extras" have an end.

And, when we leave the heated room,
　　And, when at four the lights expire,
　　The crew shall gather round the fire
And mock our laughter in the gloom.

Talk as we talked, and they ere death—
　　First wanly, dance in ghostly wise,
　　With ghosts of tunes for melodies,
And vanish at the morning's breath.

CHRISTMAS IN INDIA.

DIM dawn behind the tamarisks—the sky is
    saffron-yellow—
As the women in the village grind the corn,
And the parrots seek the river-side, each calling
    to his fellow
That the Day, the staring Eastern Day is born.
    Oh the white dust on the highway! Oh the
        stenches in the byway!
    Oh the clammy fog that hovers over earth!
    And at Home they're making merry 'neath
        the white and scarlet berry—
    What part have India's exiles in their mirth?

Full day behind the tamarisks—the sky is blue
    and staring—
As the cattle crawl afield beneath the yoke,

And they bear One o'er the field-path, who is
    past all hope or caring,
  To the ghât below the curling wreaths of smoke.
    Call on Rama, going slowly, as ye bear a
        brother lowly —
      Call on Rama—he may hear, perhaps, your
          voice!
    With our hymn-books and our psalters we
        appeal to other altars,
      And to-day we bid "good Christian men
          rejoice!"

High noon behind the tamarisks—the sun is hot
    above us —
As at Home the Christmas Day is breaking wan.
They will drink our healths at dinner—those who
        tell us how they love us,
  And forget us till another year be gone!
    Oh the toil that knows no breaking! Oh
      the *Heimweh*, ceaseless, aching!

Oh the black dividing Sea and alien Plain!
Youth was cheap — wherefore we sold it.
Gold was good — we hoped to hold it,
And to-day we know the fulness of our
gain.

Gray dusk behind the tamarisks — the parrots fly
together —
As the sun is sinking slowly over Home;
And his last ray seems to mock us shackled in
a lifelong tether
That drags us back howe'er so far we
roam.
Hard her service, poor her payment — she in
ancient, tattered raiment —
India, she the grim Stepmother of our
kind.
If a year of life be lent her, if her temple's
shrine we enter,
The door is shut — we may not look behind.

Black night behind the tamarisks — the owls
begin their chorus —
As the conches from the temple scream and
bray.
With the fruitless years behind us, and the
hopeless years before us,
Let us honor, O my brothers, Christmas Day!
Call a truce, then, to our labors — let us
feast with friends and neighbors,
And be merry as the custom of our caste;
For if "faint and forced the laughter," and
if sadness follow after,
We are richer by one mocking Christmas
past.

PAGETT, M.P.

THE toad beneath the harrow knows
Exactly where each tooth-point goes.
The butterfly upon the road
Preaches contentment to that toad.

PAGETT, M.P., was a liar, and a fluent liar
    therewith,—

He spoke of the heat of India as the "Asian
    Solar Myth;"

Came on a four months' visit, to "study the
    East," in November,

And I got him to sign an agreement vowing to
    stay till September.

March came in with the *koïl.* Pagett was cool
    and gay,

Called me a "bloated Brahmin," talked of my
    "princely pay."

March went out with the roses. "Where is
    your heat?" said he.
"Coming," said I to Pagett. "Skittles!" said
    Pagett, M. P.

April began with the punkah, coolies, and prickly-
    heat, —
Pagett was dear to mosquitoes, sandflies found
    him a treat.
He grew speckled and lumpy — hammered, I
    grieve to say,
Aryan brothers who fanned him, in an illiberal way.

May set in with a dust-storm, — Pagett went
    down with the sun.
All the delights of the season tickled him one by one.
Imprimis — ten days' "liver" — due to his drink-
    ing beer;
Later, a dose of fever — slight, but he called it
    severe.

Dysent'ry touched him in June, after the *Chota Bursat* —

Lowered his portly person — made him yearn to depart.

He didn't call me a "Brahmin," or "bloated," or "overpaid,"

But seemed to think it a wonder that any one stayed.

July was a trifle unhealthy, — Pagett was ill with fear,

'Called it the "Cholera Morbus," hinted that life was dear.

He babbled of "Eastern exile," and mentioned his home with tears;

But I hadn't seen *my* children for close upon seven years.

We reached a hundred and twenty once in the Court at noon,

(I've mentioned Pagett was portly) Pagett went off in a swoon.

That was an end to the business; Pagett, the
    perjured, fled
With a practical, working knowledge of "Solar
    Myths" in his head.

And I laughed as I drove from the station, but
    the mirth died out on my lips
As I thought of the fools like Pagett who write
    of their "Eastern trips,"
And the sneers of the travelled idiots who duly
    misgovern the land,
And I prayed to the Lord to deliver another one
    into my hand.

THE SONG OF THE WOMEN.

(Lady Dufferin's Fund for medical aid to the Women of India)

HOW shall she know the worship we would
 do her?
The walls are high, and she is very far.
How shall the women's message reach unto her
 Above the tumult of the packed bazaar?
 Free wind of March, against the lattice
 blowing,
 Bear thou our thanks, lest she depart
 unknowing.

Go forth across the fields we may not roam in,
 Go forth beyond the trees that rim the city,
To whatsoe'er fair place she hath her home in,
 Who dowered us with wealth of love and pity.

Out of our shadow pass, and seek her singing —
"I have no gifts but Love alone for bringing."

Say that we be a feeble folk who greet her,
  But old in grief, and very wise in tears;
Say that we, being desolate, entreat her
  That she forget us not in after years;
    For we have seen the light, and it were
      grievous
    To dim that dawning if our lady leave us.

By life that ebbed with none to stanch the
  failing,
  By Love's sad harvest garnered in the spring,
When Love in ignorance wept unavailing
  O'er young buds dead before their blossoming;
    By all the gray owl watched, the pale moon
      viewed,
    In past grim years, declare our gratitude!

By hands uplifted to the Gods that heard not,
By gifts that found no favor in their sight,
By faces bent above the babe that stirred not,
By nameless horrors of the stifling night;
By ills foredone, by peace her toils discover,
Bid Earth be good beneath and Heaven
above her!

If she have sent her servants in our pain,
If she have fought with Death and dulled his
sword;
If she have given back our sick again,
And to the breast the weakling lips restored,
Is it a little thing that she has wrought?
Then Life and Death and Motherhood be
nought.

Go forth, O wind, our message on thy wings,
And they shall hear thee pass and bid thee
speed,

In   reed - roofed   hut,   or   white - walled   home   of
   kings,
 Who have been helpen by her in their need.
  All spring shall give thee fragrance, and the
   wheat
  Shall be a tasselled floorcloth to thy feet.

Haste, for our hearts are with thee, take no
   rest !
 Loud - voiced ambassador, from sea to sea
Proclaim the blessing, manifold, confest,
 Of those in darkness by her hand set free,
  Then very softly to her presence move,
  And whisper: " Lady, lo, they know and
   love ! "

A BALLADE OF JAKKO HILL.

ONE moment bid the horses wait,
　　Since tiffin is not laid till three,
Below the upward path and straight
　You climbed a year ago with me.
Love came upon us suddenly
　And loosed — an idle hour to kill —
A headless, armless armory
　That smote us both on Jakko Hill.

Ah Heaven! we would wait and wait
　Through Time and to Eternity!
Ah Heaven! we could conquer Fate
　With more than Godlike constancy!
I cut the date upon a tree —
　Here stand the clumsy figures still: —
"10-7-85, A.D."
Damp with the mist on Jakko Hill.

What came of high resolve and great,
  Aud until Death fidelity ?
Whose horse is waiting at your gate ?
  Whose *'rickshaw* - wheels ride over me ?
No Saint's, I swear; and — let me see
  To - night what names your programme fill —
We drift asunder merrily,
  As drifts the mist on Jakko Hill !

L'ENVOI.

Princess, behold our ancient state
  Has clean departed ; and we see
'Twas Idleness we took for Fate
  That bound light bonds on you and me.
Amen ! Here ends the comedy
  Where it began in all good will ;
Since Love and Leave together flee
  As driven mist on Jakko Hill !

THE PLEA OF THE SIMLA DANCERS.

Too late, alas! the song
To remedy the wrong,—
The rooms are taken from us, swept and garnished for their fate.
But these tear-besprinkled pages
Shall attest to future ages
That we cried against the crime of it—too late, alas! too late!

"WHAT have *we* ever done to bear this
grudge?"
Was there no room save only in Benmore
For docket, *duftar*, and for office drudge,
    That you usurp our smoothest dancing floor?
Must babus do their work on polished teak?
    Are ball-rooms fittest for the ink you spill?
Was there no other cheaper house to seek?
    You might have left them all at Strawberry Hill.

We never harmed you! Innocent our guise,
    Dainty our shining feet, our voices low;

And we revolved to divers melodies,
  And we were happy but a year ago.
To - night, the moon that watched our lightsome
    wiles —
  That beamed upon us through the deodars —
Is wan with gazing on official files,
  And desecrating desks disgust the stars.

Nay! by the memory of tuneful nights —
  Nay! by the witchery of flying feet —
Nay! by the glamour of fordone delights —
  By all things merry, musical, and meet —
By wine that sparkled, and by sparkling eyes —
  By wailing waltz — by reckless gallop's strain —
By dim verandas and by soft replies,
  Give us our ravished ball - room back again!

Or — hearken to the curse we lay on you!
  The ghosts of waltzes shall perplex your brain,
And murmurs of past merriment pursue
  Your 'wildered clerks that they indite in vain;

And, when you count your poor Provincial
   millions,
  The only figures that your pen shall frame
Shall be the figures of dear, dear cotillions
   Danced out in tumult long before you came.

Yea! "*See Saw*" shall upset your estimates,
  "*Dream Faces*" shall your heavy heads bemuse,
Because your hand, unheeding, desecrates
   Our temple; fit for higher, worthier use.
And all the long verandas, eloquent
   With echoes of a score of Simla years,
Shall plague you with unbidden sentiment —
   Babbling of kisses, laughter, love, and tears.

So shall you mazed amid old memories stand,
  So shall you toil, and shall accomplish
   nought,
And ever in your ears a phantom Band
   Shall blare away the staid official thought.

Wherefore — and ere this awful curse be spoken,
  Cast out your swarthy sacrilegious train,
And give — ere dancing cease and hearts be
    broken —
  Give us our ravished ball - room back again !

BALLAD OF FISHER'S BOARDING-HOUSE.

THAT night, when through the mooring-chains
  The wide-eyed corpse rolled free,
To blunder down by Garden Reach
  And rot at Kedgeree,
The tale the Hughli told the shoal
  The lean shoal told to me.

'TWAS Fultah Fisher's boarding-house
  Where sailor-men reside,
And there were men of all the ports
  From Mississip to Clyde,
And regally they spat and smoked,
  And fearsomely they lied.

They lied about the purple Sea
  That gave them scanty bread,
They lied about the Earth beneath,
  The Heavens overhead,
For they had looked too often on
  Black rum when that was red.

They told their tales of wreck and wrong,
  Of shame and lust and fraud,
They backed their toughest statements with
  The Brimstone of the Lord,
And crackling oaths went to and fro
  Across the fist-banged board.

And there was Hans the blue-eyed Dane,
  Bull-throated, bare of arm,
Who carried on his hairy chest
  The maid Ultruda's charm —
The little silver crucifix
  That keeps a man from harm.

And there was Jake Without-the-Ears,
  And Pamba the Malay,
And Carboy Gin the Guinea cook,
  And Luz from Vigo Bay,
And Honest Jack who sold them slops
  And harvested their pay.

And there was Salem Hardieker,
  A lean´ Bostonian he —
Russ, German, English, Halfbreed, Finn,
  Yank, Dane, and Portugee,
At Fultah Fisher's boarding-house
  They rested from the sea.

Now Anne of Austria shared their drinks,
  Collinga knew her fame,
From Tarnau in Galicia
  To Jaun Bazar she came,
To eat the bread of infamy
  And take the wage of shame.

She held a dozen men to heel —
  Rich spoil of war was hers,
In hose and gown and ring and chain,
  From twenty mariners,
And, by Port Law, that week, men called
  Her Salem Hardieker's.

But seamen learnt — what landsmen know —
  That neither gifts nor gain
Can hold a winking Light o' Love
  Or Fancy's flight restrain,
When Anne of Austria rolled her eyes
  On Hans the blue - eyed Dane.

Since Life is strife, and strife means knife,
  From Howrah to the Bay,
And he may die before the dawn
  Who liquored out the day,
In Fultah Fisher's boarding - house
  We woo while yet we may.

But cold was Hans the blue - eyed Dane,
  Bull - throated, bare of arm,
And laughter shook the chest beneath
  The maid Ultruda's charm —
The little silver crucifix
  That keeps a man from harm.

"You speak to Salem Hardieker,
   You was his girl, I know.
I ship mineselfs to-morrow, see,
   Und round the Skaw we go,
South, down the Cattegat, by Hjelm,
   To Besser in Saro."

When love rejected turns to hate,
   All ill betide the man.
"You speak to Salem Hardieker"—
   She spoke as woman can.
A scream—a sob—"He called me—names!"
   And then the fray began.

An oath from Salem Hardieker,
   A shriek upon the stairs,
A dance of shadows on the wall,
   A knife-thrust unawares—
And Hans came down, as cattle drop,
   Across the broken chairs.

In Anne of Austria's trembling hands
 The weary head fell low : —
"I ship mineselfs to-morrow, straight
 For Besser in Saro :
Und there Ultruda comes to me
 At Easter, und I go

"South, down the Cattegat — What's here ?
 There — are — no — lights — to — guide ! "
The mutter ceased, the spirit passed,
 And Anne of Austria cried
In Fultah Fisher's boarding-house
 When Hans the mighty died.

Thus slew they Hans the blue-eyed Dane,
 Bull-throated, bare of arm,
But Anne of Austria looted first
 The maid Ultruda's charm —
The little silver crucifix
 That keeps a man from harm.

"*AS THE BELL CLINKS.*"

AS I left the Halls at Lumley, rose the vision of a comely

Maid last season worshipped dumbly, watched with fervor from afar;

And I wondered idly, blindly, if the maid would greet me kindly.

That was all — the rest was settled by the clinking tonga-bar.

Yea, my life and hers were coupled by the tonga coupling-bar.

For my misty meditation, at the second changing-station,

Suffered sudden dislocation, fled before the tuneless jar

Of a Wagner *obbligato*, *scherzo*, double-hand *staccato*,

Played on either pony's saddle by the clacking
    tonga - bar —
Played with human speech, I fancied, by the
    jigging, jolting bar.

"She was sweet," thought I, "last season, but
    'twere surely wild unreason
Such tiny hope to freeze on as was offered by
    my Star,
When she whispered, something sadly : — 'I — we
    feel your going badly!' "
"*And you let the chance escape you?*" rapped the
    rattling tonga - bar.
'*What a chance and what an idiot!*" clicked
    the vicious tonga - bar.

Heart of man — oh, heart of putty! Had I gone
    by Kakahutti,
On the old Hill - road and rutty, I had 'scaped
    that fatal car,

But his fortune each must bide by, so I
 watched the milestones slide by,
To "*You call on Her to-morrow!*" — fugue with
 cymbals by the bar —
"*You must call on Her to-morrow!*" — post-horn
 gallop by the bar.

Yet a further stage my goal on — we were whirling down to Solon,
With a double lurch and roll on, best foot fore-
 most, *ganz und gar.*—
"She was *very* sweet," I hinted. "If a kiss had
 been imprinted — ? "
"'*Would ha' saved a world of trouble!*" clashed
 the busy tonga-bar.
"'*Been accepted or rejected!*" banged and clanged
 the tonga-bar.

Then a notion wild and daring, 'spite the income
 tax's paring,
And a hasty thought of sharing — less than many
 incomes are,

Made me put a question private, you can guess
    what I would drive at.

" You must work the sum to prove it," clanked
    the careless tonga-bar.

" Simple Rule of Two will prove it," lilted back
    the tonga-bar.

It was under Khyraghaut I mused:— " Suppose
    the maid be haughty —

(There are lovers rich — and forty) — wait some
    wealthy Avatar?

Answer, monitor untiring, 'twixt the ponies twain
    perspiring ! "

" Faint heart never won fair lady," creaked the
    straining tonga-bar.

" Can I tell you ere you ask Her ? " pounded slow
    the tonga-bar.

Last, the Tara Devi turning showed the lights
    of Simla burning,

Lit my little lazy yearning to a fiercer flame by far.

As below the Mall we jingled, through my very
  heart it tingled —

Did the iterated order of the threshing tonga-
  bar —

" *Try your luck — you can't do better !* " twanged
  the loosened tonga-bar.

AN OLD SONG.

SO long as 'neath the Kalka hills
 The tonga-horn shall ring,
So long as down the Solon dip
 The hard-held ponies swing,
So long as Tara Devi sees
 The lights o' Simla town,
So long as Pleasure calls us up,
 And duty drives us down,
  If you love me as I love you,
  What pair so happy as we two?

So long as Aces take the King,
 Or backers take the bet,
So long as debt leads men to wed,
 Or marriage leads to debt,
So long as little luncheons, Love,
 And scandal hold their vogue,

While there is sport at Annandale
  Or whiskey at Jutogh,
    If you love me as I love you,
    What knife can cut our love in two?

So long as down the rocking floor
  The raving polka spins,
So long as Kitchen Lancers spur
  The maddened violins,
So long as through the whirling smoke
  We hear the oft-told tale: —
"Twelve hundred in the Lotteries,"
  And *Whatshername* for sale?
    If you love me as I love you,
    We'll play the game and win it too.

So long as Lust or Lucre tempt
  Straight riders from the course,
So long as with each drink we pour
  Black brewage of Remorse,

So long as those unloaded guns
    We keep beside the bed
Blow off, by obvious accident,
    The lucky owner's head,
      If you love me as I love you,
      What can Life kill or Death undo?

So long as Death 'twixt dance and dance
    Chills best and bravest blood,
And drops the reckless rider down
    The rotten, rain-soaked *khud,*
So long as rumors from the North
    Make loving wives afraid,
So long as Burma takes the boy
    And typhoid kills the maid,
      If you love me as I love you,
      What knife can cut our love in two?

By all that lights our daily life
    Or works our lifelong woe,

From Boileaugunge to Simla Downs
   And those grim glades below,
Where, heedless of the flying hoof
   And clamor overhead,
Sleep, with the gray langur for guard,
   Our very scornful Dead,
     If you love me as I love you,
     All Earth is servant to us two?

By Docket, Billetdoux, and File,
   By Mountain, Cliff, and Fir,
By Fan and Sword and Office-box,
   By Corset, Plume, and Spur,
By Riot, Revel, Waltz, and War,
   By Women, Work, and Bills,
By all the life that fizzes in
   The everlasting Hills,
     If you love me as I love you,
     What pair so happy as we two?

CERTAIN MAXIMS OF HAFIZ.

I.

IF It be pleasant to look on, stalled in the
packed *serai*,

Does not the Young Man try Its temper and
pace ere he buy?

If She be pleasant to look on, what does the
Young Man say?

"Lo! She is pleasant to look on, give Her to
me to-day!"

II.

Yea, though a Kafir die, to him is remitted Jehannum

If he borrowed in life from a native at sixty
per cent per annum.

III.

Blister we not for *bursati?* So when the heart is
vext,

The pain of one maiden's refusal is drowned in
the pain of the next.

IV.

The temper of chums, the love of your wife, and
    a new piano's tune —
Which of the three will you trust at the end
    of an Indian June?

V.

Who are the rulers of Ind — to whom shall we
    bow the knee?
Make your peace with the women, and men will
    make you L. G.

VI.

Does the woodpecker flit round the young *ferash?*
    Does grass clothe a new-built wall?
Is she under thirty, the woman who holds a boy
    in her thrall?

VII.

If She grow suddenly gracious — reflect. Is it
    all for thee?
The black-buck is stalked through the bullock,
    and Man through jealousy.

VIII.

Seek not for favor of women. So shall you
find it indeed.

Does not the boar break cover just when you're
lighting a weed?

IX.

If He play, being young and unskilful, for shekels
of silver and gold,

Take His money, my son, praising Allah. The
kid was ordained to be sold.

X.

With a "weed" among men or horses verily this
is the best,

That you work him in office or dog‐cart lightly
—but give him no rest.

XI.

Pleasant the snaffle of Courtship, improving the
manners and carriage;

But the colt who is wise will abstain from the
terrible thorn‐bit of Marriage.

XII.

As the thriftless gold of the *babul*, so is the
    gold that we spend
On a Derby Sweep, or our neighbor's wife, or
    the horse that we buy from a friend.

XIII.

The ways of man with a maid be strange, yet
    simple and tame
To the ways of a man with a horse, when
    selling or racing that same.

XIV.

In public Her face turneth to thee, and pleasant
    Her smile when ye meet.
It is ill. The cold rocks of El-Gidar smile
    thus on the waves at their feet.
In public Her face is averted, with anger She
    nameth thy name.
It is well. Was there ever a loser content with
    the loss of the game?

XV.

If She have spoken a word, remember thy lips are sealed,

And the Brand of the Dog is upon him by whom is the secret revealed.

If She have written a letter, delay not an instant, but burn it.

Tear it in pieces, O Fool, and the wind to her mate shall return it!

If there be trouble to Herward, and a lie of the blackest can clear,

Lie, while thy lips can move or a man is alive to hear.

XVI.

My Son, if a maiden deny thee and scufflingly bid thee give o'er,

Yet lip meets with lip at the lastward — get out! She has been there before.

They are pecked on the ear and the chin and the nose who are lacking in lore.

XVII.

If we fall in the race, though we win, the hoof-
slide is scarred on the course.
Though Allah and Earth pardon Sin, remaineth
forever Remorse.

XVIII.

"By all I am misunderstood!" if the Matron
shall say, or the Maid: —
"Alas! I do not understand," my son, be thou
nowise afraid.
In vain in the sight of the Bird is the net of
the Fowler displayed.

XIX.

My son, if I, Hafiz, thy father, take hold of thy
knees in my pain,
Demanding thy name on stamped paper, one day
or one hour — refrain.
Are the links of thy fetters so light that thou
cravest another man's chain?

THE GRAVE OF THE HUNDRED HEAD.

THERE'S a widow in sleepy Chester
  Who weeps for her only son ;
There's a grave on the Pabeng River,
  A grave that the Burmans shun,
And there's Subadar Prag Tewarri
  Who tells how the work was done.

A Snider squibbed in the jungle,
  Somebody laughed and fled,
And the men of the First Shikaris
  Picked up their Subaltern dead,
With a big blue mark in his forehead
  And the back blown out of his head.

Subadar Prag Tewarri,
  Jemadar Hira Lal,

Took command of the party,
　Twenty rifles in all,
Marched them down to the river
　As the day was beginning to fall.

They buried the boy by the river,
　A blanket over his face —
They wept for their dead Lieutenant,
　The men of an alien race —
They made a *samádh* in his honor,
　A mark for his resting-place.

For they swore by the Holy Water,
　They swore by the salt they ate,
That the soul of Lieutenant Eshmitt Sahib
　Should go to his God in state;
With fifty file of Burman
　To open him Heaven's gate.

The men of the First Shikaris
　Marched till the break of day,

Till they came to the rebel village,
  The village of Pabengmay —
A *jingal* covered the clearing,
  Calthrops hampered the way.

Subadar Prag Tewarri,
  Bidding them load with ball,
Halted a dozen rifles
  Under the village wall;
Sent out a flanking - party
  With Jemadar Hira Lal.

The men of the First Shikaris
  Shouted and smote and slew,
Turning the grinning *jingal*
  On to the howling crew.
The Jemadar's flanking - party
  Butchered the folk who flew.

Long was the morn of slaughter,
  Long was the list of slain,

Five score heads were taken,
　Five score heads and twain;
And the men of the First Shikaris
　Went back to their grave again,

Each man bearing a basket
　Red as his palms that day,
Red as the blazing village —
　The village of Pabengmay.
And the "*drip-drip-drip*" from the baskets
　Reddened the grass by the way.

They made a pile of their trophies
　High as a tall man's chin,
Head upon head distorted,
　Set in a sightless grin,
Anger and pain and terror
　Stamped on the smoke-scorched skin.

Subadar Prag Tewarri
　Put the head of the Boh

On the top of the mound of triumph,
  The head of his son below,
With the sword and the peacock-banner
  That the world might behold and know.

Thus the *samádh* was perfect,
  Thus was the lesson plain
Of the wrath of the First Shikaris —
  The price of a white man slain;
And the men of the First Shikaris
  Went back into camp again.

Then a silence came to the river,
  A hush fell over the shore,
And Bohs that were brave departed,
  And Sniders squibbed no more;
    For the Burmans said
    That a *kullah's* head
Must be paid for with heads five score.

There's a widow in sleepy Chester
Who weeps for her only son;
There's a grave on the Pabeng River,
A grave that the Burmans shun,
And there's Subadar Prag Tewarri
Who tells how the work was done.

THE MOON OF OTHER DAYS.

BENEATH the deep veranda's shade,
 When bats begin to fly,
I sit me down and watch — alas! —
 Another evening die.
Blood-red behind the sere *ferash*
 She rises through the haze.
Sainted Diana! can that be
 The Moon of Other Days?

Ah! shade of little Kitty Smith,
 Sweet Saint of Kensington!
Say, was it ever thus at Home
 The Moon of August shone,
When arm in arm we wandered long
 Through Putney's evening haze,
And Hammersmith was Heaven beneath
 The Moon of Other Days?

But Wandle's stream is Sutlej now,
  And Putney's evening haze
The dust that half a hundred kine
  Before my window raise.
Unkempt, unclean, athwart the mist
  The seething city looms,
In place of Putney's golden gorse
  The sickly *babul* blooms.

Glare down, old Hecate, through the dust,
  And bid the pie-dog yell,
Draw from the drain its typhoid-germ,
  From each bazaar its smell;
Yea, suck the fever from the tank
  And sap my strength therewith:
Thank Heaven, you show a smiling face
  To little Kitty Smith!

THE OVERLAND MAIL.

(Foot - Service to the Hills.)

IN the name of the Empress of India, make
way,
O Lords of the Jungle, wherever you roam.
The woods are astir at the close of the day —
We exiles are waiting for letters from Home.
Let the robber retreat — let the tiger turn tail —
In the Name of the Empress, the Overland
Mail!

With a jingle of bells as the dusk gathers in,
He turns to the foot - path that heads up the
hill —
The bags on his back and a cloth round his chin,
And, tucked in his waist - belt, the Post Office
bill : —

" Despatched on this date, as received by the ra.
Per runner, two bags of the Overland Mail."

Is the torrent in spate? He must ford it or
   swim.
  Has the rain wrecked the road ? He must
   climb by the cliff.
Does the tempest cry " Halt " ?   What are
   tempests to him ?
  The Service admits not a " but " or an " if."
While the breath's in his mouth, he must bear
   without fail,
In the Name of the Empress, the Overland Mail.

From aloe to rose - oak, from rose - oak to fir,
  From level to upland, from upland to crest,
From rice - field to rock - ridge, from rock - ridge to
   spur,
  Fly the soft sandalled feet, strains the brawny
   brown chest.

From rail to ravine — to the peak from the
vale —

Up, up through the night goes the Overland
Mail.

There's a speck on the hillside, a dot on the
road —

A jingle of bells on the foot-path below —

There's a scuffle above in the monkey's abode —

The world is awake, and the clouds are aglow.

For the great Sun himself must attend to the
hail : —

"In the name of the Empress, the Overland
Mail!"

WHAT THE PEOPLE SAID.

(*June 21st, 1887.*)

BY the well, where the bullocks go
    Silent and blind and slow —
By the field where the young corn dies
In the face of the sultry skies,
They have heard, as the dull Earth hears
The voice of the wind of an hour,
The sound of the Great Queen's voice :—
"My God hath given me years,
Hath granted dominion and power:
And I bid you, O Land, rejoice."

And the ploughman settles the share
More deep in the grudging clod;
For he saith: "The wheat is my care,
And the rest is the will of God.

"He sent the Mahratta spear
As He sendeth the rain,
And the *Mlech*, in the fated year,
Broke the spear in twain,
And was broken in turn. Who knows
How our Lords make strife?
It is good that the young wheat grows,
For the bread is Life."

Then, far and near, as the twilight drew,
 Hissed up to the scornful dark
Great serpents, blazing, of red and blue,
That rose and faded, and rose anew,
 That the Land might wonder and mark
"To-day is a day of days," they said,
"Make merry, O People, all!"
And the Ploughman listened and bowed his
 head:—
"To-day and to-morrow God's will," he said,
As he trimmed the lamps on the wall.

"He sendeth us years that are good,
As He sendeth the dearth.
He giveth to each man his food,
Or Her food to the Earth.
Our Kings and our Queens are afar —
On their peoples be peace —
God bringeth the rain to the Bar,
That our cattle increase."

And the Ploughman settled the share
More deep in the sun-dried clod: —
"Mogul, Mahratta, and *Mlech* from the North,
And White Queen over the Seas —
God raiseth them up and driveth them forth
As the dust of the ploughshare flies in the
    breeze;
But the wheat and the cattle are all my care,
And the rest is the will of God."

THE UNDERTAKER'S HORSE.

"To-TSCHIN-SHU is condemned to death. How can he drink tea with the Executioner?"—*Japanese Proverb.*

THE eldest son   bestrides him,
    And the pretty daughter rides him,
And I meet him oft o' mornings on the Course;
And there wakens in my bosom
An emotion chill and gruesome
As I canter past the Undertaker's Horse.

Neither shies he nor is restive,
But a hideously suggestive
Trot, professional and placid, he affects;
And the cadence of his hoof-beats
To my mind, this grim reproof beats:—
"Mend your pace, my friend, I'm coming. Who's
    the next?"

Ah! stud-bred of ill-omen,

I have watched the strongest go — men

Of pith and might and muscle — at your heels,

Down the plantain-bordered highway,

(Heaven send it ne'er be my way!)

In a lacquered box and jetty upon wheels.

Answer, sombre beast and dreary,

Where is Brown, the young, the cheery,

Smith, the pride of all his friends and half the
    Force?

You were at that last dread *dak*

We must cover at a walk,

Bring them back to me, O Undertaker's Horse!

With your mane unhogged and flowing,

And your curious way of going,

And that business-like black crimping of your
    tail,

E'en with Beauty on your back, sir,

Pacing as a lady's hack, Sir,
What wonder when I meet you I turn pale?

It may be you wait your time, Beast,
Till I write my last bad rhyme, Beast,
Quit the sunlight, cut the rhyming, drop the
　glass,
Follow after with the others,
Where some dusky heathen smothers
Us with marigolds in lieu of English grass.

Or, perchance, in years to follow,
I shall watch your plump sides hollow,
See Carnifex (gone lame) become a corse,
See old age at last o'erpower you,
And the Station Pack devour you,
I shall chuckle then, O Undertaker's Horse!

But to insult, gibe, and quest, I've
Still the hideously suggestive

Trot that hammers out the grim and warning
    text,

And I hear it hard behind me,

In what place soe'er I find me : —

"Sure to catch you sooner or later. Who's the
    next ? "

THE FALL OF JOCK GILLESPIE.

THIS fell when dinner - time was done —
    'Twixt the first an' the second rub —
That oor mon Jock cam' hame again
    To his rooms ahint the Club.

An' syne he laughed, an' syne he sang,
    An' syne we thocht him fou,
An' syne he trumped his partner's trick,
    An' garred his partner rue.

Then up and spake an elder mon,
    That held the Spade its Ace —
"God save the lad! Whence comes the licht
    That wimples on his face?"

An' Jock he sniggered, an' Jock he smiled,
    An' ower the card - brim wunk: —

"I'm a' too fresh fra' the stirrup-peg,
  May be that I am drunk."

"There's whusky brewed in Galashiels,
  An' L. L. L. forbye;
But never liquor lit the low
  That keeks fra' oot your eye.

"There's a thrid o' hair on your dress-coat breast,
  Aboon the heart a wee?"
"Oh! that is fra' the lang-haired Skye
  That slobbers ower me."

"Oh! lang-haired Skyes are lovin' beasts,
  An' terrier dogs are fair,
But never yet was terrier born
  Wi' ell-lang gowden hair!

"There's a smirch o' pouther on your breast,
  Below the left lappel?"
"Oh! that is fra' my auld cigar,
  Whenas the stump-end fell."

"Mon Jock, ye smoke the Trichi coarse,
  For ye are short o' cash,
An' best Havanas couldna leave
  Sae white an' pure an ash.

"This nicht ye stopped a story braid,
  An' stopped it wi' a curse —
Last nicht ye told that tale yoursel,
  An' capped it wi' a worse!

"Oh! we're no fou! Oh! we're no fou!
  But plainly we can ken
Ye're fallin', fallin', fra' the band
  O' cantie single men!"

An' it fell when *sirris*-shaws were sere,
  An' the nichts were lang and mirk,
In braw new breeks, wi' a gowden ring,
  Oor Jockie gaed to the Kirk.

ARITHMETIC ON THE FRONTIER.

A GREAT and glorious thing it is
    To learn, for seven years or so,
The Lord knows what of that and this,
    Ere reckoned fit to face the foe—
The flying bullet down the Pass,
That whistles clear: "All flesh is grass."

Three hundred pounds per annum spent
    On making brain and body meeter
For all the murderous intent
    Comprised in "villanous saltpetre!"
And after—ask the Yusufzaies
What comes of all our 'ologies.

A scrimmage in a Border Station—
    A canter down some dark defile—

Two thousand pounds of education
  Drops to a ten-rupee *jezail* —
The Crammer's boast, the Squadron's pride,
Shot like a rabbit in a ride!

No proposition Euclid wrote,
  No formulæ the text-books know,
Will turn the bullet from your coat,
  Or ward the tulwar's downward blow.
Strike hard who cares — shoot straight who can —
The odds are on the cheaper man.

One sword-knot stolen from the camp
  Will pay for all the school expenses
Of any Kurrum Valley scamp
  Who knows no word or moods and tenses,
But, being blessed with perfect sight,
Picks off our messmates left and right.

With home-bred hordes the hill-sides teem,
  The troop-ships bring us one by one,

At vast expense of time and steam,

  To slay Afridis where they run.

The "captives of our bow and spear"

Are cheap — alas! as we are dear.

ONE VICEROY RESIGNS.

(Lord Dufferin to Lord Lansdowne.)

SO here's your Empire. No more wine, then?
    Good.
We'll clear the Aides and *khitmatgars* away.
(You'll know that fat old fellow with the knife —
He keeps the Name Book, talks in English too,
And almost thinks himself the Government.)
O Youth, Youth, Youth! Forgive me, you're so
    young.
Forty from sixty — twenty years of work
And power to back the working. *Ay de mi!*
You want to know, you want to see, to touch,
And, by your lights, to act. It's natural.
I wonder can I help you. Let me try.
You saw — what did you see from Bombay east?
Enough to frighten any one but me?

Neat that! It frightened Me in Eighty-Four!
You shouldn't take a man from Canada
And bid him smoke in powder-magazines;
Nor with a Reputation such as — Bah!
That ghost has haunted me for twenty years,
My Reputation now full blown — Your fault —
Yours, with your stories of the strife at Home,
Who's up, who's down, who leads and who is
    led —
One reads so much, one hears so little here.
Well, now's your turn of exile. I go back
To Rome and leisure. All roads lead to Rome,
Or books — the refuge of the destitute.
When you . . . that brings me back to India.
    See!
  Start clear. I couldn't. Egypt served my turn.
You'll never plumb the Oriental mind,
And if you did it isn't worth the toil.
Think of a sleek French priest in Canada;
Divide by twenty half-breeds. Multiply

By twice the Sphinx's silence. There's your East,
And you're as wise as ever. So am I.

Accept on trust and work in darkness, strike
At venture, stumble forward, make your mark,
(It's chalk on granite), then thank God no flame
Leaps from the rock to shrivel mark and man.
I'm clear — my mark is made. Three months of
    drought
Had ruined much. It rained and washed away
The specks that might have gathered on my
    Name.
I took a country twice the size of France,
And shuttered up one doorway in the North.
I stand by those. You'll find that both will pay,
I pledged my Name on both — they're yours
    to - night.
Hold to them — they hold fame enough for two.
I'm old, but I shall live till Burma pays.
Men there — *not* German traders — Cr-sthw-te
    knows —

You'll find it in my papers.   For the North
Guns always — quietly — but always guns.
You've seen your Council ?   Yes, they'll try to
    rule,
And prize their Reputations.   Have you met
A grim lay - reader with a taste for coins,
And faith in Sin most men withhold from God ?
He's gone to England.   R–p–n knew his grip
And kicked.   A Council always has its H–pes.
They look for nothing from the West but Death
Or Bath or Bournemouth.   Here's their ground.
                                    They fight
Until the middle classes take them back,
One of ten millions plus a C. S. I.
Or drop in harness.   Legion of the Lost ?
Not altogether — earnest, narrow men,
But chiefly earnest, and they'll do your work,
And end by writing letters to the *Times.*
(Shall *I* write letters, answering H–nt–r — fawn
With R–p–n on the Yorkshire grocers ?   Ugh !)

They have their Reputations. Look to one —
I work with him — the smallest of them all,
White - haired, red - faced, who sat the plunging
  horse
Out in the garden. He's your right - hand man,
And dreams of tilting W–ls–y from the throne,
But while he dreams gives woik we cannot buy;
He nas his Reputation — wants the Lords
By way of Frontier Roads. Meantime, I think,
He values very much the hand that falls
Upon his shoulder at the Council table —
Hates cats and knows his business: *which is
  yours.*

  Your business! Twice a hundred million souls.
Your business! I could tell you what I did
Some nights of Eighty - Five, at Simla, worth
A Kingdom's ransom. When a big ship drives,
God knows to what new reef the man at the
  wheel
Prays with the passengers. They lose their lives,

Or rescued go their way; but he's no man

To take his trick at the wheel again — that's
worse

Than drowning. Well, a galled Mashobra mule

(You'll see Mashobra) passed me on the Mall,

And I was — some fool's wife had ducked and
bowed

To show the others I would stop and speak.

Then the mule fell — three galls, a hand-breadth
each,

Behind the withers. Mrs. Whatsisname

Leers at the mule and me by turns, thweet
thoul!

"How could they make him carry such a load!"

I saw — it isn't often I dream dreams —

More than the mule that minute — smoke and
flame

From Simla to the haze below. That's weak.

You're younger. You'll dream dreams before
you've done.

You've youth, that's one — good workmen — that
   means two
Fair chances in your favor. Fate's the third.
I know what *I* did.   Do you ask me, "Preach"?
I answer by my past or else go back
To platitudes of rule — or take you thus
In confidence and say : — "You know the trick :
You've governed Canada. You know. *You* know !"
And all the while commend you to Fate's hand
(Here at the top one loses sight o' God),
Commend you, then, to something more than you —
The Other People's blunders and . . . that's all.
I'd agonize to serve you if I could.
It's incommunicable, like the cast •
That drops the tackle with the gut adry.
Too much — too little — there's your salmon lost !
And so I tell you nothing — wish you luck,
And wonder — how I wonder ! — for your sake
And triumph for my own. You're young, you're
   young,

You hold to half a hundred Shibboleths.
I'm old. I followed Power to the last,
Gave her my best, and Power followed Me.
It's worth it — on my soul I'm speaking plain,
Here by the claret glasses! — worth it all.
I gave — no matter what I gave — I win.
I *know* I win. Mine's work, good work that
    live!
A country twice the size of France — the North
Safeguarded. That's my record: sink the rest
And better if you can. The Rains may serve,
Rupees may rise — three pence will give you
    Fame —
It's rash to hope for sixpence — If they rise
Get guns, more guns, and lift the salt-tax.
                        Oh!
I told you what the Congress meant or thought?
I'll answer nothing. Half a year will prove
The full extent of time and thought you'll spare
To Congress. Ask a Lady Doctor *once*

How little Begums see the light — deduce

Thence how the True Reformer's child is born.

It's interesting, curious . . . and vile.

I told the Turk he was a gentleman.

I told the Russian that his Tartar veins

Bled pure Parisian ichor; and he purred.

The Congress doesn't purr. I think it swears.

You're young — you'll swear too ere you've reached
    the end.

The End! God help you, if there be a God.

(There must be one to startle Gl–dst–ne's soul

In that new land where all the wires are cut,

And Cr–ss snores anthems on the asphodel.)

God help you! And I'd help you, if I could,

But that's beyond me. Yes, your speech was
    crude.

Sound claret after olives — yours and mine;

But Medoc slips into vin ordinaire.

(I'll drink my first at Genoa to your health.)

Raise it to Hock. You'll never catch my style.

And, after all, the middle-classes grip

The middle-class — for Brompton talk Earl's
    Court.

Perhaps you're right. I'll see you in the *Times* —

A quarter-column of eye-searing print,

A leader once a quarter—then a war;

The Strand abellow through the fog: "Defeat!"

"'Orrible slaughter!" While you lie awake

And wonder. Oh, you'll wonder ere you're free!

I wonder now. The four years slide away

So fast, so fast, and leave me here alone.

R—y, C–lv–n, L—l, R–b–rts, B–ck, the rest,

Princes and Powers of Darkness, troops and
    trains,

(I *cannot* sleep in trains), land piled on land,

Whitewash and weariness, red rockets, dust,

White snows that mocked me, palaces — with
    draughts,

And W–stl–nd with the drafts he couldn't pay,

Poor W–ls–n reading his obituary

Before he died, and H–pe, the man with bones,
And A–tch–s–n a dripping mackintosh
At Council in the Rains, his grating "Sirrr"
Half drowned by H–nt–r's silky: — "Bát my
    lahd."
Hunterian always: M–rsh–l spinning plates
Or standing on his head; the Rent Bill's roar,
A hundred thousand speeches, much red cloth,
And Smiths thrice happy if I call them Jones,
(I can't remember half their names) or reined
My pony on the Mall to greet their wives.
More trains, more troops, more dust, and then
    all's done.
Four years, and I forget. If I forget
How will *they* bear me in their minds? The
    North
Safeguarded — nearly (R–b–rts knows the rest),
A country twice the size of France annexed.
That stays at least. The rest may pass — may
    pass —

Your heritage — and I can teach you nought.

"High trust," "vast honor," "interests twice as
    vast,"

"Due reverence to your Council" — keep to those.

I envy you the twenty years you've gained,

But not the five to follow. What's that? One?

Two! — Surely not so late. Good-night. *Don't*
    dream.

THE BETROTHED.

"You must choose between me and your cigar."

OPEN the old cigar-box, get me a Cuba stout,
For things are running crossways, and Maggie
and I are out.

We quarrelled about Havanas — we fought o'er a
good cheroot,
And I know she is exacting, and she says I am
a brute.

Open' the old cigar-box — let me consider a
space ;
In the soft blue veil of the vapor, musing on
Maggie's face.

Maggie is pretty to look at — Maggie's a loving
    lass,
But the prettiest cheeks must wrinkle, the truest
    of loves must pass.

There's peace in a Laranaga, there's calm in a
    Henry Clay,
But the best cigar in an hour is finished and
    thrown away —

Thrown away for another as perfect and ripe
    and brown —
But I could not throw away Maggie for fear o'
    the talk o' the town!

Maggie, my wife at fifty — gray and dour and
    old —
With never another Maggie to purchase for love
    or gold!

And the light of Days that have Been the dark
    of the Days that Are,
And Love's torch stinking and stale, like the
    butt of a dead cigar —

The butt of a dead cigar you are bound to keep
    in your pocket —
With never a new one to light tho' it's charred
    and black to the socket.

Open the old cigar-box — let me consider a
    while —
Here is a mild Manilla — there is a wifely
    smile.

Which is the better portion — bondage bought
    with a ring,
Or a harem of dusky beauties fifty tied in a
    string ?

Counsellors cunning and silent — comforters true
　　and tried,

And never a one of the fifty to sneer at a rival
　　bride.

Thought in the early morning, solace in time of
　　woes,

Peace in the hush of the twilight, balm ere my
　　eyelids close.

This will the fifty give me, asking nought in
　　return,

With only a *Suttee's* passion — to do their duty
　　and burn.

This will the fifty give me. When they are
　　spent and dead,

Five times other fifties shall be my servants
　　instead.

The furrows of far-off Java, the isles of the
    Spanish Main,
When they hear my harem is empty, will send
    me my brides again.

I will take no heed to their raiment, nor food
    for their mouths withal,
So long as the gulls are nesting, so long as the
    showers fall.

I will scent 'em with best vanilla, with tea will
    I temper their hides,
And the Moor and the Mormon shall envy who
    read of the tale of my brides.

For Maggie has written a letter to give me my
    choice between
The wee little whimpering Love and the great
    god Nick o' Teen.

And I have been servant of Love for barely a
twelvemonth clear,

But I have been Priest of Partagas a matter of
seven year;

And the gloom of my bachelor days is flecked
with the cheery light

Of stumps that I burned to Friendship and
Pleasure and Work and Fight.

And I turn my eyes to the future that Maggie
and I must prove,

But the only light on the marshes is the Will-
o'-the-Wisp of Love.

Will it see me safe through my journey, or
leave me bogged in the mire?

Since a puff of tobacco can cloud it, shall I
follow the fitful fire?

Open the old cigar-box — let me consider anew —
Old friends, and who is Maggie that I should
    abandon *you?*

A million surplus Maggies are willing to bear
    the yoke;
And a woman is only a woman, but a good
    cigar is a Smoke.

Light me another Cuba; I hold to my first-sworn
    vows,
If Maggie will have no rival, I'll have no
    Maggie for spouse!

A TALE OF TWO CITIES.

WHERE the sober-colored cultivator smiles
On his *byles;*
Where the cholera, the cyclone, and the crow
Come and go;
Where the merchant deals in indigo and tea,
Hides and *ghi;*
Where the Babu drops inflammatory hints
In his prints;
Stands a City — Charnock chose it — packed away
Near a Bay —
By the sewage rendered fetid, by the sewer
Made impure,
By the Sunderbunds unwholesome, by the swamp
Moist and damp;
And the City and the Viceroy, as we see,
Don't agree.

Once, two hundred years ago, the trader came
        Meek and tame.
Where his timid foot first halted, there he
    stayed,
        Till mere trade
Grew to Empire, and he sent his armies forth
        South and North
Till the country from Peshawar to Ceylon
        Was his own.
Thus the mid-day halt of Charnock — more's the
    pity !
        Grew a City.
As the fungus sprouts chaotic from its bed,
        So it spread —
Chance-directed, chance-erected, laid and built
        On the silt —
Palace, byre, hovel — poverty and pride —
        Side by side ;
And, above the packed and pestilential town,
        Death looked down.

But the Rulers in that City by the Sea
        Turned to flee —
Fled, with each returning spring-tide from its ills
        To the Hills.
From the clammy fogs of morning, from the
    blaze
        Of the days,
From the sickness of the noontide, from the heat,
        Beat retreat;
For the country from Peshawar to Ceylon
        Was their own.
But the Merchant risked the perils of the Plain
        For his gain.

Now the resting-place of Charnock, 'neath the
    palms,
        Asks an alms,
And the burden of its lamentation is,
        Briefly, this : —
"Because, for certain months, we boil and stew,
        So should you.

Cast the Viceroy and his Council, to perspire
>   In our fire!"
And for answer to the argument, in vain
>   We explain
That an amateur Saint Lawrence cannot fry:—
>   "*All* must fry!"
That the Merchant risks the perils of the Plain
>   For his gain.
Nor can Rulers rule a house that men grow
>   rich in,   .
>   From its kitchen.

Let the Babu drop inflammatory hints
>   In his prints;
And mature—consistent soul—his plan for steal-
>   ing
>   To Darjeeling:
Let the Merchant seek, who makes his silver pile,
>   England's isle;
Let the City Charnock pitched on—evil day!—
>   Go Her way.

Though the argosies of Asia at Her doors
   Heap their stores,
Though Her enterprise and energy secure
   Income sure,
Though "out-station orders punctually obeyed"
   Swell Her trade —
Still, for rule, administration, and the rest,
   Simla's best.

GRIFFEN'S DEBT.

IMPRIMIS he was "broke."   Thereafter left
   His regiment, and, later, took to drink;
Then, having lost the balance of his friends,
"Went Fantee" — joined the people of the land,
Turned three parts Mussulman and one Hindu,
And lived among the Gauri villagers,
Who gave him shelter and a wife or twain,
And boasted that a thorough, full-blood *sahib*
Had come among them.   Thus he spent his
   time,
Deeply indebted to the village *shroff*,
(Who never asked for payment) always drunk,
Unclean, abominable, out-at-heels;
Forgetting that he was an Englishman.

You know they dammed the Gauri with a dam,
And all the good contractors scamped their work,

And all the bad material at hand
Was used to dam the Gauri — which was cheap,
And, therefore, proper. Then the Gauri burst,
And several hundred thousand cubic tons
Of water dropped into the valley, *flop,*
And drowned some five and twenty villagers,
And did a lakh or two of detriment
To crops and cattle. When the flood went down
We found him dead, beneath an old dead horse,
Full six miles down the valley. So we said
He was a victim to the Demon Drink,
And moralized upon him for a week,
And then forgot him. Which was natural.

But, in the valley of the Gauri, men
Beneath the shadow of the big new dam
Relate a foolish legend of the flood,
Accounting for the little loss of life
(Only those five and twenty villagers)
In this wise: On the evening of the flood,

They heard the groaning of the rotten dam,
And voices of the Mountain Devils. Then
An incarnation of the local God,
Mounted upon a monster-neighing horse,
And flourishing a flail-like whip, came down,
Breathing ambrosia, to the villages,
And fell upon the simple villagers
With yells beyond the power of mortal throat,
And blows beyond the power of mortal hand,
And smote them with the flail-like whip, and
    drove
Them clamorous with terror up the hill,
And scattered, with the monster-neighing steed,
Their crazy cottages about their ears,
And generally cleared those villages.
Then came the water, and the local God,
Breathing ambrosia, flourishing his whip,
And mounted on his monster-neighing steed,
Went down the valley with the flying trees
And residue of homesteads, while they watched

Safe on the mountain-side these wondrous things,
And knew that they were much beloved of
    Heaven.

Wherefore, and when the dam was newly built,
They raised a temple to the local God,
And burned all manner of unsavory things
Upon his altar, and created priests,
And blew into a conch, and banged a bell,
And told the story of the Gauri flood
With circumstance and much embroidery.

So he the whiskified Objectionable,
Unclean, abominable, out-at-heels,
Became the tutelary Deity
Of all the Gauri valley villages;
And may in time become a Solar Myth.

IN SPRINGTIME.

MY garden blazes brightly with the rose - bush
and the peach,
  And the *köil* sings above it, in the *siris* by
  the well,
From the creeper - covered trellis comes the squir-
rel's chattering speech,
  And the blue - jay screams and flutters where
  the cheery *sat - bhai* dwell.
But the rose has lost its fragrance, and the
köil's note is strange;
  I am sick of endless sunshine, sick of blossom-
  burdened bough.
Give me back the leafless woodlands where the
winds of Springtime range —
  Give me back one day in England, for it's
  Spring in England now!

Through the pines the gusts are booming, o'er
    the brown fields blowing chill,
  From the furrow of the ploughshare streams
    the fragrance of the loam,
And the hawk nests on the cliff-side and the
    jackdaw in the hill,
  And my heart is back in England mid the
    sights and sounds of Home.
But the garland of the sacrifice this wealth of
    rose and peach is;
  Ah! *köil*, little *köil*, singing on the *siris*
    bough,
In my ears the knell of exile your ceaseless
    bell-like speech is—
  Can *you* tell me aught of England or of
    Spring in England now?

TWO MONTHS.

IN JUNE.

NO hope, no change! The clouds have shut
      us in
  And through the cloud the sullen Sun strikes
      down
  Full on the bosom of the tortured Town.
Till Night falls heavy as remembered sin
That will not suffer sleep or thought of ease.
   And, hour on hour, the dry-eyed Moon in spite
   Glares through the haze and mocks with
        watery light
The torment of the uncomplaining trees.

Far off, the Thunder bellows her despair
To echoing Earth, thrice parched. The lightnings
   fly

In vain. No help the heaped-up clouds afford,
But wearier weight of burdened, burning air.
What truce with Dawn? Look, from the aching
    sky,
Day stalks, a tyrant with a flaming sword!

IN SEPTEMBER.

At dawn there was a murmur in the trees,
    A ripple on the tank, and in the air
    Presage of coming coolness — everywhere
A voice of prophecy upon the breeze.
Up leapt the sun and smote the dust to gold,
    And strove to parch anew the heedless land,
All impotently, as a King grown old
    Wars for the Empire crumbling 'neath his
    hand.

One after one, the lotos - petals fell,
Beneath the onslaught of the rebel year

In mutiny against a furious sky;
And far-off Winter whispered: "It is well!
Hot Summer dies. Behold, your help is near,
For when men's need is sorest, then come I."

THE GALLEY-SLAVE.

OH, gallant was our galley from her carven
steering-wheel
To her figurehead of silver and her beak of
hammered steel;
The leg-bar chafed the ankle, and we gasped for
cooler air,
But no galley on the water with our galley
could compare!

Our bulkheads bulged with cotton and our masts
were stepped in gold —
We ran a mighty merchandise of niggers in the
hold;
The white foam spun behind us, and the black
shark swam below,
As we gripped the kicking sweep-head and we
made that galley go.

It was merry in the galley, for we revelled now
    and then —
If they wore us down like cattle, faith, we
    fought and loved like men!
As we snatched her through the water, so we
    snatched a minute's bliss,
And the mutter of the dying never spoiled the
    lovers' kiss.

Our women and our children toiled beside us in
    the dark —
They died, we filed their fetters, and we heaved
    them to the shark —
We heaved them to the fishes, but so fast the
    galley sped,
We had only time to envy, for we could not
    mourn our dead.

Bear witness, once my comrades, what a hard-
    bit gang were we —
The servants of the sweep - head, but the masters
    of the sea!

By the hands that drove her forward as she
    plunged and yawed and sheered,
Woman, Man, or God or Devil, was there any-
    thing we feared?

Was it storm? Our fathers faced it, and a
    wilder never blew;
Earth that waited for the wreckage watched the
    galley struggle through.
Burning noon or choking midnight, Sickness,
    Sorrow, Parting, Death?
Nay, our very babes would mock you, had they
    time for idle breath.

But to-day I leave the galley, and another takes
    my place;
There's my name upon the deck-beam — let it
    stand a little space.
I am free — to watch my messmates beating out
    to open main,
Free of all that Life can offer — save to handle
    sweep again.

By the brand upon my shoulder, by the gall of
    clinging steel,
By the welt the whips have left me, by the
    scars that never heal;
By eyes grown old with staring through the
    sun-wash on the brine,
I am paid in full for service — would that ser-
    vice still were mine!

Yet they talk of times and seasons and of woe
    the years bring forth,
Of our galley swamped and shattered in the
    rollers of the North.
When the niggers break the hatches, and the
    decks are gay with gore,
And a craven-hearted pilot crams her crashing
    on the shore.

She will need no half-mast signal, minute-gun,
    or rocket-flare,
When the cry for help goes seaward, she will
    find her servants there.

Battered chain-gangs of the orlop, grizzled drafts
    of years gone by,
To the bench that broke their manhood, they
    shall lash themselves and die.

Hale and crippled, young and aged, paid, deserted,
    shipped away —
Palace, cot, and lazaretto shall make up the tale
    that day,
When the skies are black above them, and the
    decks ablaze beneath,
And the top-men clear the raffle with their
    clasp-knives in their teeth.

It may be that Fate will give me life and leave
    to row once more —
Set some strong man free for fighting as I take
    awhile his oar.
But to-day I leave the galley. Shall I curse
    her service then ?
God be thanked — whate'er comes after, I have
    lived and toiled with Men !

L'ENVOI.

(To whom it may concern.)

THE smoke upon your Altar dies,
　The flowers decay,
The Goddess of your sacrifice
　Has flown away.
What profit then to sing or slay
The sacrifice from day to day?

"We know the Shrine is void," they said,
　"The Goddess flown —
Yet wreaths are on the Altar laid —
　The Altar - Stone
Is black with fumes of sacrifice,
Albeit She has fled our eyes.

"For, it may be, if still we sing
　And tend the Shrine,

Some Deity on wandering wing
  May there incline;
And, finding all in order meet,
Stay while we worship at Her feet."

THE CONUNDRUM OF THE WORKSHOPS.

WHEN the flush of a new-born sun fell first
    on Eden's green and gold,
Our father Adam sat under the Tree and scratched
    with a stick in the mould;
And the first rude sketch that the world had
    seen was joy to his mighty heart,
Till the Devil whispered behind the leaves: "It's
    pretty, but is it art?"

Wherefore he called to his wife, and fled to
    fashion his work anew —
The first of his race who cared a fig for the
    first, most dread review;
And he left his lore to the use of his sons —
    and that was a glorious gain
When the Devil chuckled: "Is it art?" in the
    ear of the branded Cain.

They builded a tower to shiver the sky and
    wrench the stars apart,
Till the Devil grunted behind the bricks: "It's
    striking, but is it art?"
The stone was dropped by the quarry-side, and
    the idle derrick swung,
While each man talked of the aims of art, and
    each in an alien tongue.

They fought and they talked in the north and the
    south, they talked and they fought in the west,
Till the waters rose on the jabbering land, and
    the poor Red Clay had rest—
Had rest till the dank blank-canvas dawn when
    the dove was preened to start,
And the Devil bubbled below the keel: "It's
    human, but is it art?"

The tale is old as the Eden Tree—as new as
    the new-cut tooth—
For each man knows ere his lip-thatch grows
    he is master of art and truth;

And each man hears as the twilight nears, to
 the beat of his dying heart,
The Devil drum on the darkened pane: "You
 did it, but was it art?"

We have learned to whittle the Eden Tree to
 the shape of a surplice - peg,
We have learned to bottle our parents twain in
 the yolk of an addled egg,
We know that the tail must wag the dog, as
 the horse is drawn by the cart;
But the Devil whoops, as he whooped of old:
 "It's clever, but is it art?"

When the flicker of London sun falls faint on
 the club - room's green and gold,
The sons of Adam sit them down and scratch
 with their pens in the mould —
They scratch with their pens in the mould of their
 graves, and the ink and the anguish start
When the Devil mutters behind the leaves: "It's
 pretty, but is it art?"

Now, if we could win to the Eden Tree where
    the four great rivers flow,
And the wreath of Eve is red on the turf as
    she left it long ago,
And if we could come when the sentry slept,
    and softly scurry through,
By the favor of God we might know as much
    —as our father Adam knew.

THE EXPLANATION.

LOVE and Death once ceased their strife
　　At the Tavern of Man's Life.
Called for wine, and threw — alas ! —
Each his quiver on the grass.
When the bout was o'er they found
Mingled arrows strewed the ground.
Hastily they gathered then
Each the loves and lives of men.
Ah, the fateful dawn deceived !
Mingled arrows each one sheaved :
Death's dread armory was stored
With the shafts he most abhorred :
Love's light quiver groaned beneath
Venom - headed darts of Death.

Thus it was they wrought our woe
At the Tavern long ago.
Tell me, do our masters know,
Loosing blindly as they fly,
Old men love while young men die?

THE GIFT OF THE SEA.

THE dead child lay in the shroud,
   And the widow watched beside;
And her mother slept, and the Channel swept
  The gale in the teeth of the tide.

But the widow laughed at all.
   "I have lost my man in the sea,
And the child is dead. Be still," she said,
  "What more can ye do to me?"

And the widow watched the dead,
   And the candle guttered low,
And she tried to sing the Passing Song
  That bids the poor soul go.

And "Mary take you now," she sang,
   "That lay against my heart."
And "Mary smooth your crib to-night,"
   But she could not say "Depart."

Then came a cry from the sea,
   But the sea-rime blinded the glass,
And "Heard ye nothing, mother?" she said;
   "'Tis the child that waits to pass."

And the nodding mother sighed.
   "'Tis a lambing ewe in the whin,
For why should the christened soul cry out,
   That never knew of sin?"

"Oh, feet I have held in my hand,
   Oh, hands at my heart to catch,
How should they know the road to go,
   And how should they lift the latch?"

They laid a sheet to the door,
  With the little quilt atop,
That it might not hurt from the cold or the
    dirt,
  But the crying would not stop.

The widow lifted the latch   .
  And strained her eyes to 'see,
And opened the door on the bitter shore
  To let the soul go free.

There was neither glimmer nor ghost,
  There was neither spirit nor spark,
And "Heard 'ye nothing, mother?" she said,
  " 'Tis crying for me in the dark."

And the nodding mother sighed.
  " 'Tis sorrow makes ye dull;
Have ye yet to learn the cry of the tern,
  Or the wail of the wind-blown gull?"

"The terns are blown inland,
　The gray gull follows the plough.
'Twas never a bird, the voice I heard,
　O mother, I hear it now!"

"Lie still, dear lamb, lie still;
　The child is passed from harm,
'Tis the ache in your breast that broke your
　　rest,
　And the feel of an empty arm."

She puts her mother aside,
　"In Mary's name let be!
For the peace of my soul I must go," she said,
　And she went to the calling sea.

In the heel of the wind-bit pier,
　Where the twisted weed was piled,
She came to the life she had missed by an hour,
　For she came to a little child.

She laid it into her breast,
  And back to her mother she came,
But it would not feed, and it would not heed,
  Though she gave it her own child's name.

And the dead child dripped on her breast,
  And her own in the shroud lay stark;
And, "God forgive us, mother," she said,
  "We let it die in the dark!"

EVARRA AND HIS GODS.

Read here,

This is the story of Evarra — man —

Maker of Gods in lands beyond the sea.

Because the city gave him of her gold,

Because the caravans brought turquoises,

Because his life was sheltered by the King,

So that no man should maim him, none should
    steal,

Or break his rest with babble in the streets

When he was weary after toil, he made

An image of his God in gold and pearl,

With turquoise diadem and human eyes,

A wonder in the sunshine, known afar

And worshipped by the King; but, drunk with
    pride,

Because the city bowed to him for God,

He wrote above the shrine: "*Thus Gods are*
    made,
And whoso makes them otherwise shall die."
And all the city praised him. . . . Then he died.

Read here the story of Evarra — man —
Maker of Gods in lands beyond the sea.
  Because his city had no wealth to give,
  Because the caravans were spoiled afar,
  Because his life was threatened by the King,
  So that all men despised him in the streets,
  He hacked the living rock, with sweat and
    tears,
  And reared a God against the morning-gold,
  A terror in the sunshine, seen afar,
  And worshipped by the King; but, drunk with
    pride,
  Because the city fawned to bring him back,
  He carved upon the plinth: "*Thus Gods are*
    made,

And whoso makes them otherwise shall die."

And all the people praised him. . . . Then he
    died.

Read here the story of Evarra — man —
Maker of Gods in lands beyond the sea.

Because he lived among a simple folk,

Because his village was between the hills,

Because he smeared his cheeks with blood of
    ewes,

He cut an idol from a fallen pine,

Smeared blood upon its cheeks, and wedged a
    shell

Above its brows for eye, and gave it hair

Of trailing moss, and plaited straw for crown.

And all the village praised him for this craft,

And brought him butter, honey, milk, and curds.

Wherefore, because the shoutings drove him mad,

He scratched upon that log: *" Thus Gods are*
    made,

And whoso makes them otherwise shall die."

And all the people praised him. . . . Then he
    died.

Read here the story of Evarra — man —
Maker of Gods in lands beyond the sea.

Because his God decreed one clot of blood
Should swerve a hair's-breadth from the pulse's
    path,
And chafe his brain, Evarra mowed alone,
Rag-wrapped, among the cattle in the fields,
Counting his fingers, jesting with the trees,
And mocking at the mist, until his God
Drove him to labor. Out of dung and horns
Dropped in the mire he made a monstrous God,
Abhorrent, shapeless, crowned with plaintain tufts.
And when the cattle lowed at twilight-time,
He dreamed it was the clamor of lost crowds,
And howled among the beasts: *" Thus Gods*
    are made,

And whoso makes them otherwise shall die."
Thereat the cattle bellowed. . . . Then he died.

Yet at the last he came to Paradise,
And found his own four Gods, and that he wrote;
And marvelled, being very near to God,
What oaf on earth had made his toil God's law,
Till God said, mocking: "Mock not. These be
    thine."
Then cried Evarra: "I have sinned!"—"Not so.
If thou hadst written otherwise, thy Gods
Had rested in the mountain and the mine,
And I were poorer by four wondrous Gods,
And thy more wondrous law, Evarra. Thine,
Servant of shouting crowds and lowing kine."
Thereat with laughing mouth, but tear-wet eyes,
Evarra cast his Gods from Paradise.
This is the story of Evarra—man—
Maker of Gods in lands beyond the sea.